HEGEMON GROUP INTERNATIONAL

LEADERSHIP FORMAT SYSTEM
The Blueprint For Success

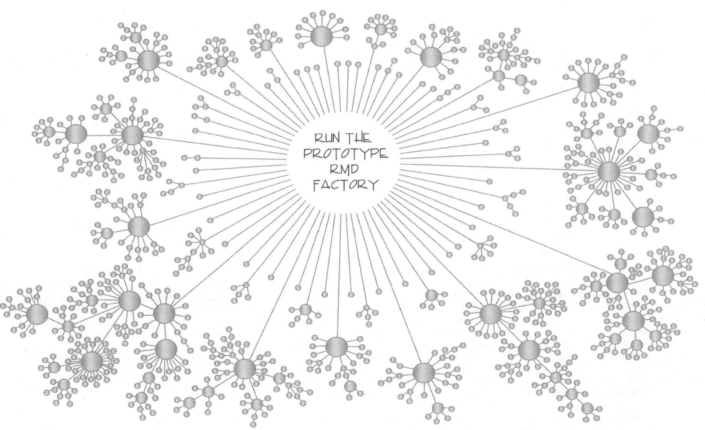

RUN THE PROTOTYPE RMD FACTORY

YOU RUN THE SYSTEM AND THE SYSTEM BUILDS YOUR BUSINESS.

The LFS Manual is composed of 3 Main Sections...
Leadership Section I is Recruiters Mentality
Leadership Section II is Builders Mindset
Leadership Section III is Director of Motivation.

Hegemon Group International is pleased to provide this training manual to you, as an independent contractor and associate of this company. As you know, Hegemon Group International, in conjunction with other companies, makes products available to you, for sale to the public. Although there are various sales position designations among Hegemon Group International's sales force, product inventory is not distributed or sold to Hegemon Group International's sales force. In addition, independent contractors are not required to purchase any products, goods, services, inventory, marketing plan or property of any kind, or pay any consideration in exchange for becoming an independent contractor and associate of this company. However, all new independent contractors have to pay an administrative service fee to cover the costs of processing your application, performing background checks, coordinating the salesperson paperwork, etc. Finally, the compensation you will earn, if any, will depend solely upon your personal efforts, and hard work. While many people have experienced successful careers within Hegemon Group International, this success represents individual associate member experiences. As each individual differs, so will his/her specific results. Work ethic patterns, activity levels and dedication all play significant roles in determining the outcome that one may achieve and in his/her ability to control his/her destiny on an ongoing basis. This statement is not intended to nor does it represent that any current member's individual results are representative of what all participants achieve when following the Hegemon Group International system. There is no compensation or consideration earned by independent contractors in exchange for encouraging others to join Hegemon Group International's sales force.

Hegemon Group International is not a franchise operation. We simply provide the master copy of a proven system for you to duplicate. Again, you are an independent contractor in business for yourself. The ideas and guidelines expressed in this manual are not mandatory, but are merely suggestions based on what has worked in the past. You have the freedom to build your business within the framework of your contractual agreement with Hegemon Group International and its affiliated companies. However, always remember that alignment creates velocity. Hegemon Group International is built upon the "Team Over Me" principle, and there is great synergy in people moving together.

We are proud of this training manual and make it available to you for educational and training purposes only. Illustrations in the manual of how recruiting others to join Hegemon Group International's sales force can affect commissions of independent contractors and associates are not a representation of past or projected future earnings of independent contractors.

No statement, illustration, graph or other representation in the training manual is intended to form a contractual agreement or to modify or to supplement any existing contractual agreement between Hegemon Group International and you. The terms and provisions of any contractual agreements between you and Hegemon Group International and commission rates are found in the HGI Associate Membership Agreement and any other addendums thereto.

For training and educational purposes only. Not to be used with the public.

2

Introduction

History tells us that many times founders and innovators lack the vision they need to achieve total greatness.

Nowhere is this more evident than in the early days of the great Coca-Cola company.

In 1885, John Pemberton, an Atlanta pharmacist, produced a tonic, French Wine Cola, rather similar to Coca-Cola. Pemberton carried a jug of it down the street to Jacobs' Pharmacy where, on Saturday, May 8, 1886, it was sold for the first time, for five cents a glass.

Pemberton, however, had limited success, selling only 25 gallons of syrup in his first year. Pemberton spent more money on advertising than he actually earned.

Just before his death in 1888, Pemberton sold his remaining interest in Coca-Cola to Asa G. Candler, the only one who understood the drink and its fabulous potential, for a mere $1,200.

On January 29, 1892, along with his brother and a couple of friends, Candler founded the original Coca-Cola Company. By 1916, Candler was 65 years old, and when he retired as president of the company. By focusing exclusively on soda fountain sales, he had become one of the country's great commercial success stories. But even Candler didn't have the vision for what would turn Coca-Cola into a worldwide giant in the bottling business.

Two young, enterprising attorneys, however, did have the ability to look to the future. Benjamin Thomas and Joseph Whitehead went to Candler with their idea to bottle Coca-Cola nationwide.

The result surpassed their wildest dreams - Candler sold them the rights to bottle Coca-Cola in almost the entire U. S. for the meager sum of one dollar (that he never cashed).

Candler, a member of an older generation who simply did not have the vision for the progress of the new century, never grasped the importance of the operation that would make Coca-Cola famous.

Hegemon Group International's Leadership Format System is to marketing what the bottling business was to Cola-Cola.

Don't make the same mistake Asa Candler did. Take Napoleon Hill's advice: "If you want to be a millionaire, find one and do exactly as he does."

Now, you can copy HGI's turnkey system detailed in this Leadership Format System manual. It explains in a simple, straightforward step-by-step process, everything you need to know to build your HGI business, by copying HGI's greatest Leaders and duplicating their success.

In addition to the Leadership Format System manual, you can study the online version at LFSMAX.com/LFSmanual. You will find additional study resources including embedded audios and videos that provide unique insights into the fine points of running the pure building system.

In marketing, one big idea can change everything. Turnkey Marketing is it in the 21st century.

For training and educational purposes only. Not to be used with the public.

7

Introduction

The Turnkey Revolution

Everyone knows the impact that the Industrial Revolution, the Technological Revolution and the Information Explosion have had on our lives. At the heart of the Turnkey Revolution is a way of doing business that has the power to dramatically transform any company from a condition of chaos to a condition of order, excitement and continuous growth. It's the key to the development of a successful business - the ultimately balanced model of a business that works.

Now, as a direct by-product of the Turnkey Revolution, HGI's turnkey Leadership Format System will allow you to put the magic of multiples to work for you.

"Id rather have 1% of the efforts of 100 men than 100% of my own efforts."
- J. Paul Getty

The Franchise Phenomenon

(Editors Note - Since HGI is not a franchise and does not sell franchises, all discussion of franchises is merely conceptual as it relates to HGI.)

It all started in 1952 when a 52-year-old salesman walked into a hamburger stand in California. He was looking to sell a milk shake machine. Instead, he witnessed a miracle. No one knew it yet, but the Turnkey Revolution had been launched.

Ray Kroc, the salesman, had never seen anything like the MacDonald brothers' hamburger stand.

Hamburgers were being cranked out quickly, efficiently, inexpensively, and, most importantly, identically. High school students, under the strict supervision of the owners, responded to the long lines of customers like clockwork.

That was the best thing about the system - anyone could do it. Kroc saw the very first MacDonald's (later, of course, McDonald's) for what it really was - not a hamburger stand, but a money machine.

Twelve years and millions of burgers later, Kroc bought out the MacDonald brothers and went on to create the largest retail prepared food distribution system in the world. Today, McDonald's serves 6% of the U.S. population every single day.

One of the most profitable retail businesses in the world, McDonald's remains the model upon which an entire generation of entrepreneurs have since built their fortunes - the franchise phenomenon.

But the genius of McDonald's isn't franchising itself. The true genius of McDonald's is the Business Format Franchise. It is the Business Format Franchise that has revolutionized American business, and is the key to understanding the Turnkey Revolution. Even though HGI does not sell franchises, the franchise system is one key to understanding Turnkey Marketing and the future success of your career.

Introduction

Turning the Key: The Business Format Franchise

The Business Format Franchise moves a step beyond simply using the company trade name. The Business Format Franchise also provides the franchisee with an entire system of doing business. Therein lies the foundation of the Turnkey Revolution, and the success of those who have studied and copied it.

The Business Format Franchise is built upon the belief that the true product of a business is not what it sells, but how it sells it. The true product of a business is the business itself.

Ray Kroc understood from the very beginning that the hamburger wasn't his product, McDonald's was.

Problem: Huge Dreams/No Money

Ray Kroc once suffered from the same problems as many other entrepreneurs, past and present. He had huge dreams and very little money.

Solution = HGI

The franchisee became Kroc's vehicle to realize his dreams; the recruit can become yours.

Kroc began to look at the business as his product. The franchisee didn't care about burgers, fries and milk shakes - all he was interested in was the business. The franchisee had only one concern: "Does it work?"

Your recruits will have the same question.

Opportunity Must Be Better Than Any Other

Kroc knew that in order for him to realize his dreams, McDonald's had to work better than anything else out there. That, in turn, would create more demand.

Kroc realized he wasn't competing with other hamburger stands. He was competing with every other business (and so are we, in HGI).

Must Work Every Time, No Matter Who

There was another critical reason why Kroc had to make certain McDonald's would work. He knew that he couldn't leave the operation of the business in the hands of the franchisees, for they would certainly blow it.

Fool-Proof, Predictable and Profitable

The problem became the opportunity.

The business had to work in order to be sold, and it had to work once it was sold - no matter who bought it. The results: a fool-proof, predictable and profitable business.

Work on Business, Not in Business

Ray Kroc went to work on his business, not in it. That's what you must learn to do with HGI.

Introduction

Prototype

He began to think about his business like an engineer would who was working on a pre-production prototype of a mass-producible product. The prototype had to be constructed so that the resulting business system could be replicated over and over and over again - each business working as reliably as the thousands that preceded it.

Once developed, the prototype had to be tested and perfected long before ever going into mass production.

That is the secret to the Business Format Franchise, the Franchise Prototype. It is the model you must have to make your business work.

A Perfectly Running Model

During the last 30 years, HGI's Leadership team developed the prototype in which we perfected the Leadership Format System.

During this time all assumptions were put to the test to determine if they would work before they actually became operational as part of the business. Without this prototype, HGI becomes just another business, vulnerable to all of the pitfalls.

The System Runs the Business, You Run the System

Once the prototype is complete, the Leader then turns to the new associate and shows him how it works. And it does work.

The system runs the business. The people run the system.

The system is the solution to all the problems. It turns the business into a machine and drives it toward the objective. Discipline, standardization and order are critical to the system.

A rigorous training program must be completed before the McDonald's franchisee is ever allowed to operate the franchise. McDonald's has Hamburger U. McDonald's doesn't teach people how to make hamburgers – but how to run the system that makes the hamburgers - the system by which McDonald's makes its customers happy every time. That system is the foundation of McDonald's incredible success.

Once the franchisee learns the system, he has the key to his own business - a turnkey operation.

The franchisee obtains the business, learns how to run it and then "turns the key." The business takes it from there - and the franchisee loves it. In a well-designed business, every problem has been well thought-out and solved in advance. All the franchisee has to do is learn how to manage the system.

Again, even though HGI is not a franchise - and does not sell franchises - we have applied this principle so that the HGI Leadership Format System can run your business.

Introduction

Our Challenge to You

- **Dare to Dream Again**

  Because of the power of our turnkey system, you can crank up your dream machine again. Many people have either given up on their dreams or they've shrunk them down to match their incomes. Here, you can begin to dream bigger dreams and change forever your family's financial situation, and the situations of the people you bring into business with you. At HGI, you provide the dreams, and we provide the vehicle.

- **Increase Your Will to Win**

  Everyone has within them the need to compete. HGI provides you with a forum in which career and competition go hand in hand as you aspire to take advantage of our great recognition and reward system.

- **Align Yourself with HGI's System Builders**

  This is a new endeavor for you. Your challenge is to apply the system as it was set down before you. Turn yourself into the perfect copy machine. With cookie-cutter exactness, run our system over and over again, and you can achieve the same success other HGI Leaders have enjoyed. Remember, you are paid to imitate, not create.

- **Develop a Passion for Our Mission**

  The Leaders of HGI are 100% committed to creating wealth for families. There is a critical need for the education that HGI delivers on a giant scale. You'll never realize the full potential of HGI if all that motivates you is the money. Personal success is just a secondary gain - a nice payoff, but not the real prize. The real prize is being a major force behind HGI's movement to create wealth for families. Your success for the most part will depend on how strong your passion is for our mission and how effectively you can get many other people to feel the same way. It's a **mission that motivates.**

- **Run "The Play"**

  The best way to maximize the HGI opportunity and take advantage of the revolutionary Infinity Compensation & Recognition Plan is to run "The Play."

  Every new person must immediately be armed with 10 Brochures/Video Links (HGIPlay.com). Each person should experience a minimum 20% success rate and recruit at least two new people. The rapid, relentless repetition of the new Supercharged Video Drop System will ignite the greatest recruiting explosion in the history of world business.

  "The Play" will be the catalyst for helping hundreds of thousands of families worldwide realize their dreams and position HGI to Recruit the Planet.

  HGI gives you the Vision, the Mission and the System. Now, it's up to you to <u>Dream It</u> and <u>Do It</u>.

For training and educational purposes only. Not to be used with the public.

11

The Leadership Format System

The rapid relentless repetition of these 6 recruiting steps
can lead to the building of a giant distribution system.

The Continuous Opening of Outlets
The LFS 6 Steps

STEP 1 Prospecting
- **Leader** controls prospect list development.
- **Leader** paints a picture of how the team will be built.

STEP 2 The Approach/Contact
- **Leader** controls the point of contact.
- **Leader** helps start the Video Drop System/"The Play"

STEP 3 The Presentation
- **Leader** runs the Business Opportunity Presentation (BOP).
- Mozone converts the prospects.

STEP 4 The Follow-Up
- **Leader** guides new Associate through Speed Filters 1-4.

STEP 5 The Start-Up
- **Leader** gets new Associate off to a Fast Start by quickly completing Speed Filters 5-8.

STEP 6 Duplication
- **Leader** gets new Associate through the entire LFS Success Cycle over and over again.

The Simultaneous Production Through the Outlets
The Eight Speed Filters

The Follow-Up Process
(Complete Filters 1-4 within first 24-48 hours.)

FILTER 1 Stay after the Meeting

FILTER 2 Get a Decision Kit

FILTER 3 Set a Get Started Interview

FILTER 4 Keep Appointment & Sign Up

The Start-Up Process
(Complete Filters 5-8 within next 24-48 hours.)

FILTER 5 Develop a Prospect List [Step 1]

FILTER 6 Set Goals/Create Business Plan [Find the "Why"]

FILTER 7 Do Financial Needs Analysis [FNA] Internal Consumption As Needed

FILTER 8 Match-Up with Field Builder to Qualify for Associate Promotion

The Leadership Format System Flow Chart

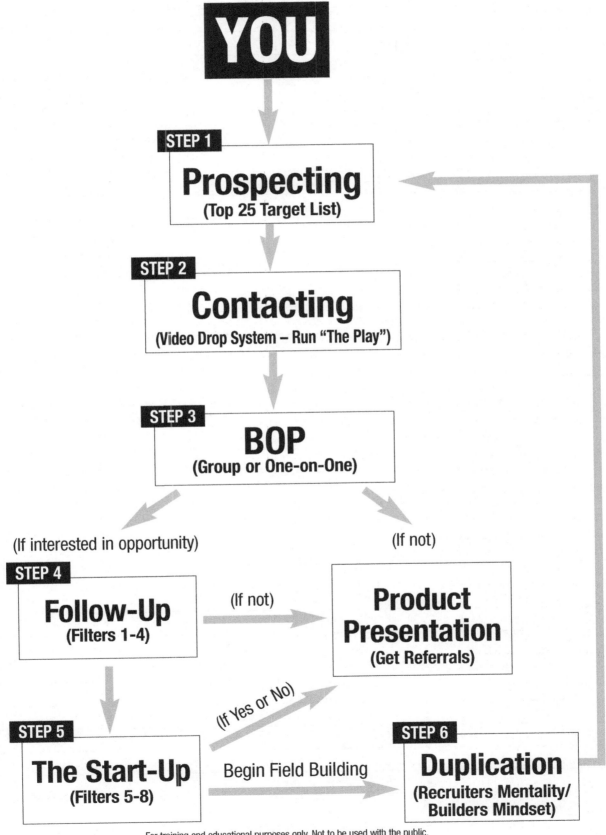

YOU

STEP 1
Prospecting
(Top 25 Target List)

STEP 2
Contacting
(Video Drop System – Run "The Play")

STEP 3
BOP
(Group or One-on-One)

(If interested in opportunity)   (If not)

STEP 4
Follow-Up
(Filters 1-4)

(If not)

Product Presentation
(Get Referrals)

(If Yes or No)

STEP 5
The Start-Up
(Filters 5-8)

Begin Field Building

STEP 6
Duplication
(Recruiters Mentality/ Builders Mindset)

For training and educational purposes only. Not to be used with the public.

Notes:

Step 1 Prospecting

Developing A Target Market

Purpose: To max-out and organize your available resources to attract the people necessary to accomplish your goals.

PROSPECTING

Just as a building contractor cannot construct a building without a large supply of raw materials, a Hegemon Group International empire builder needs a large pool of prospects to plug into the system to build a distribution empire.

You can divide prospecting into five areas:

I. Natural Market

- Friends, neighbors, relatives, co-workers, social contacts, business contacts
- Anybody and everybody

II. Friendship Farming

- Turning strangers into friends to create a new natural market
- Nobody can show how much you know until they know how much you care.

III. Friendship Borrowing System

- Relationship marketing through our third-party referral system

IV. Prospecting for Industry Professionals

- Using HGI-approved videos, ads, letters, the HGI website, etc... to expand your prospecting tools.
- Life Insurance
- Annuities
- Property & Casualty
- Registred Rep. Advisors
- Securities Reps
- Mortgage Brokers
- Real Estate Agents

V. Social Networking Through Social Media

- Facebook
- Twitter
- MySpace
- LinkedIn
- YouTube
- Google +
- Pinterest
- Live Journal
- Tagged
- Instagram
- CafeMom
- Ning
- Meetup
- MyLife
- My Yearbook

I. Natural Market

Create a Target Market List

Making a target market list should be a top priority of any new associate.

Make the list the start of an exciting business adventure. From this list, you will build a business and potentially transform the lives of the people on it.

Important Keys to Developing Your Prospect List:

1. **Never make your list on your own.**

    Complete your prospect list with your Leader, and make sure to involve your spouse when possible.

2. **Add names, don't eliminate them.**

    Resist the tendency to eliminate people from your list because you think they're too busy or make too much money. That is a major mistake. Remember, it's not just who you know, but who they know also.

3. **Use the "Executive Memory Jogger."**

    The purpose is to "jog" your memory for every quality person you know.

4. **Identify the "Top 25" on your list.**

    Your list should have a minimum of 100 names to start and grow to as many as 300 or even 500. But once you develop your list, you need to quickly identify the "Top 25" and begin contacting them immediately with your Leader. The people on your "Top 25" list should have the following general qualifications:

    - **30+ years old**

    - **Married**

    - **Dependent children**

    - **Homeowner**

    - **Solid business/career background**

    - **$40,000+ household income**

    - **Dissatisfied**

    - **Ambitious**

Memory Jogger

1. Work With	63. Teacher	125. Handball With	187. Runs Track	248. Orthodontist
2. Boss	64. Substitute Teacher	126. Swim With	188. Basketball	249. Dance Teacher
3. Partner	65. Banker	127. Fire Chief	189. Plays With Kids	250. Loves Seafood
4. Elevator Person	66. Teller	128. Fireman	190. Climbs Mountains	251. Wears Contacts
5. Landlord	67. Policeman	129. Volunteer Firefighter	191. Hang Glides	252. Computer Repair
6. Security Guard	68. Highway Patrol	130. Scout Master	192. Karate	253. Computer Sales
7. Vending Sales	69. Home Builder	131. Den Leader	193. Your Principal	254. Cabinet Master
8. Secretary	70. Painter	132. Barber	194. Your Teacher	255. Bookkeeper
9. Typing Pool	71. Roofer	133. Beautician	195. Your Coach	256. Architect
10. Caterer	72. Insulator	134. Auctioneer	196. Kid's Principal	257. Best Fund Raiser
11. Customer	73. Landscaper	135. Sells Siding	197. Kid's Teacher	258. Tree Surgeon
12. Parking Attendant	74. Wallpaper Hanger	136. Family Pictures	198. Kid's Coach	259. Railroad Conductor
13. Coffee Shop	75. Carpet Layer	137. Photographer	199. Music Teacher	260. Game Warden
14. Car Pool	76. Hospital Worker	138. Guidance Counselor	200. Piano Teacher	261. Cab Driver
15. Personal Manager	77. Department Store	139. Youth Director	201. Hates To Lose	262. Bus Driver
16. Sales People	78. Grocery Store	140. Sister-In-Law	202. Loves To Compete	263. Cat Lover
17. Boss's Lunch	79. Convenience Store	141. Brother-In-Law	203. Lamaze Class	264. Dog Lover
18. Lunch With	80. Waitress	142. Father-In-Law	204. Kiwanis	265. Animal Trainer
19. Competition	81. Waiter	143. Mother-In-Law	205. Lions Club	266. Doll Maker
20. Repair Person	82. Chef	144. Brother	206. Rotary	267. Direct Sales
21. Copier Person	83. Cashier	145. Sister	207. Good Cook	268. Social Worker
22. Union	84. Dishwasher	146. Father	208. Friend's Parents	269. Makes Good Fudge
23. Complainer	85. Auto Supply	147. Mother	209. Lawyer	270. Health Food Shop
24. Inspector	86. Electrician	148. Cousin	210. Highway Department	271. Seamstress
25. Credit Union	87. Hardware Store	149. Aunt	211. Professor	272. Bookworm
26. Pension Plan	88. Truck Driver	150. Uncle	212. Sunday School Teacher	273. Likes To Sing
27. Fired-Up Male	89. Pharmacist	151. Grandfather	213. Child's Sunday	274. Likes To Eat
28. Fired-Up Female	90. Funeral Director	152. Grandmother	School Teacher	275. Lawn Maintenance
29. Delivery Person	91. Flower Shop	153. Niece	214. Chamber of Commerce	276. Cellular Phone
30. Express Mail	92. Health Spa	154. Nephew	215. Hotel Business	277. Rotisserie League
31. U.P.S.	93. Restaurant Business	155. Best Friend	216. Printer	278. Satellite TV
32. Mailman	94. Dry Cleaner	156. Spouse's Best Friend	217. Surveyor	279. Internet
33. Lost Job	95. Electronics Store	157. Farmer	218. Radio Announcer	280. Computer Whiz
34. Almost Lost Job	96. TV Repair	158. Army	219. Sportscaster	281. E-Mail List
35. Will Be Laid Off Next	97. Furniture Repair	159. Navy	220. Writer	282. Voice-Mail List
36. Has Been Laid Off	98. Movie Rental	160. Air Force	221. Journalist	283. On-Line Service
37. Job Hunting Male	99. Appliance Person	161. Marines	222. Editor	284. Laptop Computers
38. Job Hunting Female	100. Cable TV	162. Baby-Sitter	223. Publisher	285. Software
39. Hates Job	101. Eye Center	163. Sister's In-Laws	224. Tanning Salon	286. Computer Games
40. Missed Last Promotion	102. Tire Store	164. Neighbor On Right	225. Arcade	287. Desktop Publishers
41. Walking Encyclopedia	103. Realtor	165. Neighbor On Left	226. Baker	288. Travel Agent
42. Most Likable	104. Office Supplies	166. Across Street	227. Librarian	289. Trainer
43. Needs Part-Time Job	105. Copier Salesperson	167. Behind	228. Accountant	290. Works Out With
44. Engineer	106. Vacuum Cleaner	168. Down Street	229. Machine Shop	291. Gym Members
45. New Employee	107. Phone Installer	169. Parent's Right	230. Paints Billboards	292. Club Members
46. Operator	108. Pest Control	170. Parent's Left	231. Pilot	293. Facebook
47. Payroll	109. Cosmetic Sales	171. Best Man	232. Stewardess	294. Twitter
48. Contractor	110. Carpet Cleaners	172. Maid Of Honor	233. Steward	295. MySpace
49. Movers/Shakers	111. Golf Pro	173. Matron Of Honor	234. Air Traffic Control	296. Linked In
50. Guard	112. Appliance Repair person	174. Bridesmaids	235. Ambulance Driver	297. YouTube
51. Preacher	113. Bowl With	175. Ushers	236. Travel Agent	298. Google +
52. Nurse	114. Hunt With	176. Fellow Church Members	237. Antique Dealer	299. Pinterest
53. Dentist	115. Golf With	177. Plumber	238. Armored Car	300. Live Journal
54. Doctor	116. Fish With	178. Jaycees	239. Telephone Operator	301. Tagged
55. Surgeon	117. Tennis With	179. Play Bridge	240. Piano Tuner	302. Instagram
56. Chiropractor	118. Ski With	180. Play Bingo	241. Service Station	303. Cafemom
57. Therapist	119. Throw Darts With	181. Table Tennis	242. Sign Painter	304. Ning
58. Carpenter	120. Softball With	182. Pool	243. Who You Camp With	305. Meetup
59. Auto Mechanic	121. Baseball With	183. Trivial Pursuit	244. Locksmith	306. My Life
60. Car Sales	122. Football With	184. Monopoly	245. Upholsterer	307. My Yearbook
61. Body Repair	123. Soccer With	185. Rides With	246. Veterinarian	308. Badoo
62. Gas Station	124. Racquetball With	186. Jogs	247. Notary Public	

HGI™
HEGEMON GROUP INTERNATIONAL

TOP 25 TARGET MARKET LIST

Date: _____
Associate: _____
RMD: _____

	Name	Spouse	F/A[1]	Home Number	Office Number	Profile[2]	Contact Date	Results	BOP	MA[3]	Data	Client
1												
2												
3												
4												
5												
6												
7												
8												
9												
10												
11												
12												
13												
14												
15												
16												
17												
18												
19												
20												
21												
22												
23												
24												
25												

[1] (F) Friend/(A) Acquaintance
[2] Profile (1) 30+ Years, (2) Married, (3) Dependent Children, (4) Homeowner, (5) Solid Business/Career Background, (6) $40,000+ Household Income, (7) Dissatisfied
[3] Membership Agreement Signed and Fees Paid

II. Friendship Farming

The System to Turn Strangers Into Friends

As you go about your normal daily routine, be on the look-out for people with whom to start a conversation. Study the following example, then use this approach to cultivate a new warm market by meeting new people.

Simulated Shopping Example

- Any smart shopper will look around for the best price, talk to salespeople to obtain all the facts and compare the best products on the market. Salespeople expect the "I'll be back" mentality, which creates competition and is the foundation for the way we do business in our country today.

- By playing off this mentality, you can go into any retail store, any time, any place and have a reason to talk to people using the F.O.R.M. method.

- Every morning, millions of people potentially go to work for you. They rise early, fight the traffic and position themselves in 8-10 hour blocks waiting for you to come see them.

- Best of all, they are being paid by their employer to be nice and courteous to you. If you execute this system the right way, these people will listen to you and respond to what you're doing.

- No matter where you meet someone, keep in mind the basic recruiting principles and never "spook" the person. Avoid the "Scenario of Disaster." Your goal is to get the person to attend the BOP, or worst case visit your Business Builder Web Site

The F.O.R.M. Method

There are four questions you can ask when talking with a stranger. This is called the F.O.R.M. Method. This method flows more naturally if you "prime the pump" first by sharing some personal information about yourself.

F Stands for **"Family."** You might ask him (or her) if he is a family man, does he have kids, did he grow up here in town, etc.?

O Stands for **"Occupation."** What does he do for a living? How long? Does he like his job?

R Stands for **"Recreation."** Perhaps you have a common recreational interest.

M Stands for **"Message."** Tell the prospect what you do to spark his interest. Get his name (ask for a business card) to call or drop in on him in the future and share the rest of the story.

If during the F.O.R.M. Method they ask you what you do, a good response is "I'm putting together a marketing team for an exciting new company that is expanding in this area." Don't go into any further details. Remember, you must avoid the "Scenario of Disaster."

III. Friendship Borrowing: HGI's Referral/Lead System

Most people in marketing who aren't experiencing the level of success they desire usually don't lack for a good presentation or a timely concept. What they are missing is qualified people to get in front of on a regular, consistent basis.

Many companies today rely on running ads, lead lists, mass mailings, e-mail solicitations and telemarketing to get new clients. Most people either ignore or become annoyed with these unsolicited attempts to sell them a product or service. The costs for these types of methods continue to skyrocket, while the success ratio remains very low. HGI believes there is a better way.

Relationship Marketing has proven to be the most effective way to get a product to market. Warm market referrals are not only very successful, but also extremely cost effective. You must have a system of getting and using referrals. It must not be personality driven or vary from situation to situation. It must give the associate the confidence to follow through each time, which will generate successful results, and it must be easy to duplicate.

Referrals can be asked for during any one of the steps in the system, including The Approach/Contact, The Business Opportunity Presentation, The Get Started Interview/Follow-Up, The Product Presentation, and during On-going Client Contact.

The HGI Referral/Lead System

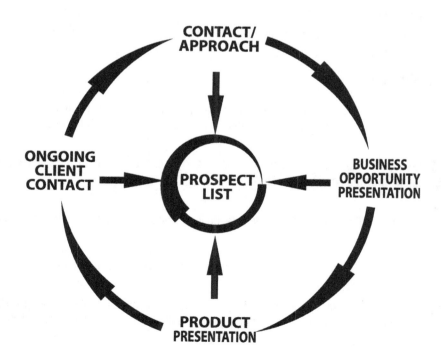

III. Friendship Borrowing: HGI's Referral/Lead System *(continued)*

Why Master the HGI Referral System?

The key to mastering the HGI Referral system is getting referrals from satisfied clients. Starting with the very first sale, here's what one serious business person can do by using the referral system:

No. Sales	No. Referrals* (10 per Sale)	Close (50-percent Ratio)
1	10	5
5	50	25
25	250	125
125	1,250	625
625	6,250	3,125

* Referrals from the client are more valuable to you than the commission on the sale.

IV. Professional Prospecting

Another way to build your business is by using the many powerful communication tools available through HGI:

- HGI contact video
  See Step 2, The Approach/Contact (page 29)
- HGI's Personal Website Packages
  See Section III, Director of Motivation (page 181)
- Approved prospecting scripts and letters
  See Step 1, Prospecting (Harvesting Referrals, next page)
- Approved advertisements
  See Section III, Director of Motivation (page 183)

V. Social Media

With the reach and effectiveness of Social Media ever increasing, HGI recognizes the tremendous benefit social media provides the company in helping to reach people with our message. HGI is embracing the latest in cutting edge social media marketing strategies, including demographic targeting, keyword marketing, lead generation as well as various training tools, and we are continually developing new strategies to utilize social networks to further expand our great mission.

In addition to Facebook, Twitter, Google+ and other various social networks, another valuable social media tool is a Google Hangout. A Google Hangout is a simple tool that allows you to interact with up to 10 people at a time through video and also allows you to share your screen so others can see your presentation. For sophisticated users, you can broadcast your Hangout live on a YouTube Channel where it can be viewed by thousands. Other tools such as Skype, Zoom, Periscope, Blab.im and others are being developed regularly. Work with your team to use these tools to hold your virtual meetings. Check HGIUniversity.com for the latest online meeting and collaboration tools.

Harvesting Referrals

The Approach/Contact

Once the approach has been made, even if the prospect is not interested in attending a BOP or Product Presentation Meeting, there is still an opportunity to obtain referrals.

"I appreciate how you feel, but let me ask you a quick question before we get off the phone: I've found my best new associates come through referrals from quality people like yourself. Who do you know that may be interested in getting involved in a new business venture or a possible career change?"

The Business Opportunity Presentation

If the prospect has attended the BOP (whether at the office or one-on-one) and is not interested in joining, there is still an opportunity to get referrals.

"I appreciate getting to meet with you today. As you can tell, our concepts can make a huge difference in someone's life. _____, I work strictly on referrals. Would you be kind enough to write down the names of a few people who might benefit from our concepts?"

The Product Presentation

The Product Presentation is the best time to get referrals. Once they have seen the power of our concepts and products, they realize this is information that everyone needs to hear.

After completing the product presentation, go ahead and get referrals.

"As you can tell, these concepts will have a dramatic impact on your financial future. The amazing part is that most people don't realize that these concepts even exist. Who do you know that at least needs to have a chance to hear about these concepts so they can have the same opportunity you did?"

For training and educational purposes only. Not to be used with the public.

22

Harvesting Referrals *(continued)*

On-Going Client Contact

Anytime you have follow-up contact with your clients, you are continuing to build your relationship with them as well as creating opportunities to get new referrals. No matter how much time has passed, your clients have met new people who need to hear about our concepts.

"Hello, this is _____. How are you? As I promised when we met, I'm calling to check and see if your financial picture has changed or if you need any help from me."

Wait For Answer (WFA)

"I appreciate the opportunity of doing business with you. I love sharing our concepts because of the impact they have on people's lives.

"As you know I work through referrals and I do not want to burden you again by asking for a list of names, but I would ask you to encourage your friends and business associates to give me a call. I'd love to show them the power of the concepts we're offering.

"Thanks again, and if you need anything please feel free to give me a call."

Overcoming Objections in the Referral/Lead System

Here are the 3 most common objections in trying to get referrals:

1. Some clients feel uncomfortable that they may upset their friends and relatives.
This comes mostly from typical over-aggressive sales people who are too pushy in the sales process. It is important for you to let them know that if the referrals are not interested in meeting that you will not pressure them in any way. Due to the potential impact our concepts and products could have on their financial future, these people should at least have the opportunity to hear about them.

2. Some clients tend to rule out certain people based on their own judgment.
It is important that your clients know that you have the capability of providing the products and services to people who are both above and below their own financial status. It is important to tell your clients not to prejudge anyone.

3. Clients feel like they don't know anyone to refer.
It's possible that they cannot think of anyone at the moment. Most people know more people than they realize once they think about it. This is where the Memory Jogger sheet from Step 1 of the LFS comes in handy to help refresh their memory. Once you master overcoming objections, you will truly have a successful turn-key referral/lead system.

Harvesting Referrals (continued)
Contacting the New Referral

There are two effective methods for contacting new referrals:

Method No. 1 – Phone Contact

"Hello, _____, this is _____. I'm a friend of _____. I recently shared a concept with _____ and _____ that they were really excited about. They were kind enough to mention that you might be interested in this concept as well. There are two ways that work best for me to share this information with you. I can either set an appointment to come by and see you at your home, or we have a group presentation on Tuesday night at 7:30 at our office. Which of these two ways works best for you?"

(WFA)

Set a time for the appointment or give them directions to the office or volunteer to pick them up.

If the prospect wants to know more before committing to meet, invite them to visit your Business Builder website and tell them you will follow up in the next few days to answer any questions.

Method No. 2 – Letter Contact

Once your client has signed the referral letter (found on the next page) and it has been mailed, it is time to follow up with a phone call.

"Hello, _____, this is _____. I'm a friend of _____. I recently shared a business concept with _____ and _____ that they were really excited about. Did you get the letter they sent to you? They were very excited about our company and our business opportunity, and were kind enough to mention that you might be interested in hearing more about it. There are two ways that work best for me to share this information with you. I can either set an appointment to come by and see you at your home, or we have a group presentation on Tuesday night at 7:30 at our office. Which of these two ways works best for you?

Harvesting Referrals (continued)

Dear _____,

Every now and then, an idea comes along that can really help us. But, in our daily rush to get things done we sometimes ignore it.

As Americans, we are concerned about our family's financial future and we are looking for ideas that makes sense and will allow us to make more money.

Recently, I met someone with answers, _____. They showed me a powerful, new business concept that has become important to me financially, especially in these uncertain times. It's a common sense plan that most people don't even know exists.

I have asked that they call you. Naturally, you will have to make up your own mind, but I am confident that a meeting will be more than worth the time you spend.

Sincerely,

P.S. I know you're busy, but I promise you'll want to learn more about this.

(Handwrite personal note and include Secrets of Money Brochure)
Example:

"Read the Brochure and watch
the videos at HGIPlay.com"

Harvesting Referrals *(continued)*

Referral Selection Form

Associate _____ Date _____

Client Name _____ Phone _____

Address _____ City _____ State _____ Zip _____

Name_____ Address _____
Spouse Name_____ Telephone _____
Age_____Work _____ Earnings _____
Children/Ages _____
Key Info. _____
Best Time_____ Nickname _____

Name_____ Address _____
Spouse Name_____ Telephone _____
Age_____Work _____ Earnings _____
Children/Ages _____
Key Info. _____
Best Time_____ Nickname _____

Name_____ Address _____
Spouse Name_____ Telephone _____
Age_____Work _____ Earnings _____
Children/Ages _____
Key Info. _____
Best Time_____ Nickname _____

Name_____ Address _____
Spouse Name_____ Telephone _____
Age_____Work _____ Earnings _____
Children/Ages _____
Key Info. _____
Best Time_____ Nickname _____

Name_____ Address _____
Spouse Name_____ Telephone _____
Age_____Work _____ Earnings _____
Children/Ages _____
Key Info. _____
Best Time_____ Nickname _____

Harvesting Referrals *(continued)*

The HGI Power Sweep

Our version of the Green Bay Packers Power Sweep is Friendship Borrowing: HGI's Referral/Lead System.
Here's what one associate can do personally starting with just one sale and getting 10 referrals from each sale.

No. of Sales	No. of Referrals (10 per Sale)	Close (50% Ratio)	Average Earnings ($2,000 commission)
1	10	5	$10,000
5	50	25	$50,000
25	250	125	$250,000
125	1,250	625	$1,250,000
625	6,250	3,125	$6,250,000

1st Month — 25 New Referrals
Initial Contact — See 15 of the 25
Results: 5 Sales x 10 Referrals =   50
              3 Recruits x 25 Referrals =   75
                        > 125 Referrals

2nd Month — 125 New Referrals
2nd phase contact — See 75 of the 125
Results: 25 Sales x 10 Referrals =   250
              15 Recruits x 25 Referrals =   375
                        > 625 Referrals

3rd Month — 625 New Referrals
3rd phase contact — See 375 of the 625
Results: 125 Sales x 10 Referrals =   1,250
              75 Recruits x 25 Referrals =   1,875
                        > 3,125 Referrals

Final results at end of 90 days: 155 Sales and 93 New Recruits

Become a master of the HGI Referral/Lead System and teach it to all your Leaders so that you may constantly
be put in front of good quality people who need to hear about our opportunity and powerful concepts and products.
It is a major key to your Leaders making money and building huge, successful organizations.

These are hypothetical situations for illustrative purposes only. There are no guarantees, but the harder you work, the greater your chances for success.

Notes:

_____
_____
_____
_____
_____
_____
_____
_____
_____
_____
_____
_____
_____
_____
_____
_____
_____
_____
_____
_____
_____
_____
_____
_____
_____
_____
_____
_____
_____
_____
_____
_____

Step 2 | The Approach/Contact

Controlling the Point of Contact

Purpose: To effectively contact a prospect and set a date to attend the next Business Opportunity Presentation (BOP) at the office, or alternatively, a One-on-One BOP in the next 24-48 hours.

THE APPROACH/CONTACT

There are two proven methods you can use in the approach/contact phase. The key is choosing the most effective method given the circumstances, and the nature of the prospect you're trying to approach.

• The Video Drop System/"The Play"

The most effective way to contact new prospects about the HGI opportunity is the Video Drop System. Utilize the most powerful recruiting tool ever known — "*The Secrets of Money*" Brochure and the video link, HGIPlay.com — to run "*The Play*" and take HGI's Video Drop System to an entirely new level.

• The Invitation Script

Using HGI's time-tested approach, you can effectively contact your natural market while avoiding the "Scenario of Disaster." You must master the art of becoming a mobile inviter.

For training and educational purposes only. Not to be used with the public.

29

Section I — RECRUITERS MENTALITY

Controlling the Point of Contact

Mastering the Video Drop System/"The Play" and a quality "Invitation Script" are the proven methods of avoiding the "Scenario of Disaster." Remember, you must control the point of contact.

"Scenario of Disaster"

➤ Your **Enthusiasm**
➤ Creates **Curiosity**
➤ They **Ask Questions**
➤ You attempt to **Answer Questions**
➤ You **Answer Wrong!!!!**
  (From incorrect or incomplete information)
➤ They **Jump to Conclusions**
➤ The result is **Failure!!!**

Become a Student of Human Nature

When inviting, you have to understand people. You have to know what turns them "on" and what turns them "off." You have to take their feelings into account and, like a fisherman or hunter, understand the nature of the beast, and be careful not to spook them.

Remember the basics about most people:

1. They're quick to jump to conclusions.
2. They're skeptical - they suffer from the "shaft" syndrome.
3. They procrastinate - the spirit is willing but the flesh is weak.
4. They dream of great wealth.
5. They're curious.
6. They don't think they can sell.
7. They don't like salespeople.
8. They would like to be their own boss.
9. They would like to have a business of their own, BUT...
10. ...they all doubt that they ever could or would.

Points to Remember in Making Contact:

1) **Show enthusiasm.**
Don't be tentative. We have a first-class, professional, quality company.

2) **Don't get into extensive questions and answers.**
For you, it's premature. Let them hear it from our experienced Leadership.

3) **Bring the person to the meeting yourself.**
Arrange to pick them up, meet at a neutral site or give clear directions to your office..

4) **Whenever possible, invite both the husband and wife.**
They are both decision makers.

5) **Master the Video Drop System/"The Play" and the Invitation Script.**
This gives you the verbal tools to effectively communicate who we are and what we do.
Learn to be a mobile inviter.

The New Supercharged Video Drop System/"The Play"

The Key: Run "The Play"

The best way to maximize the HGI opportunity and take advantage of the revolutionary Infinity Compensation & Recognition Plan is to run "The Play."

Every new person must immediately be armed with 10 powerful HGI brochures/video links (hgiplay.com). Each person should experience a minimum 20% success rate and recruit at least two new people. The rapid, relentless repetition of the new Supercharged Video Drop System will ignite the greatest recruiting explosion in the history of world business.

"The Play" will be the catalyst for helping hundreds of thousands of families worldwide realize their dreams and position HGI to Recruit the Planet.

The Video Drop System helps solve many of the problems in contacting prospects:

- You don't go out alone (the company's key Leaders are with you).
- You don't have to make a presentation.
- You don't answer questions, the brochure and video link (hgiplay.com) will do that.

This is the powerful method Hubert Humphrey used to orchestrate his greatest recruiting months ever in his field era. Hubert's massive team recruited nearly 50,000 new associates by dropping almost 150,000 brochures/video links in 90 days.

Why Master the HGI Video Drop?

One associate using the brochure/video links (hgiplay.com) and the LFS:

Cycle	People	10 Brochures	Move Twice	Recruit 20 percent
1	1	10	20	4
2	5	50	100	20
3	25	250	500	100
4	125	1,250	2,500	500
5	625	6,250	12,500	2,500

This example shows closing only External Usage (EU) sales on half of the 80 percent non-recruits who saw the brochure/video:

Cycle	People	10 Brochures	Move Twice	Half of 80 percent
1	1	10	20	8
2	5	50	100	40
3	25	250	500	200
4	125	1,250	2,500	2,000
5	325	6,250	12,500	10,000

This is a hypothetical scenario for illustrative purposes only. There is no assurance that these results can or will be achieved. Cycles represent each distribution of brochures/Videos.

The New Supercharged Video Drop System Flow

Pre-Drop Preparation:

- Train your team how to run the Video Drop System.
- Arm your team with 10 HGI brochures and video link flyers (hgiplay.com) each.
- Be prepared to arm every new recruit with 10 HGI brochures, video link flyer (hgiplay.com) and an LFS Manual.
- Have a game plan for distributing the brochures/video link flyer (hgiplay.com).
- Group your prospects geographically to save time.
- Your main goal should be to get 10 brochures with video links out ASAP following the system.
- The best way to execute the actual brochure/video links drop is to do so unannounced.
  If you feel the need to call them, do so from your cell phone when you are just minutes away from their home.
- Remember the only thing you need to tell people in response to any questions they may ask is, "Just read the brochure and watch the videos." Don't get into any other details with them. Avoid the "Scenario of Disaster" at all costs.
- It is also important to go ahead and schedule the time with your Leader to do the Three-Way Teleconferencing Follow-Up within 24-48 hours after you do the drop.

The Video Drop:

You can't fail. How complicated is it? You drop the brochure/video link invitation (hgiplay.com) off if they're home. If they are not home you drop it off anyway.

1. **Show Enthusiasm** — Body language is everything.

2. **The Entrance Line** — "I am so excited. This brochure and video are about a company that is doing fabulous things to help people and has the greatest income potential of any business I have ever seen. You just have to read the brochure and watch this video."

3. **Hand them the brochure and flyer containing the video link (hgiplay.com).**

4. **The Exit Line** — "I know you want to know more, but I don't have the time right now. Read the brochure and watch the video and I will get back with you in the next 24-48 hours, unless you get back with me first. Thanks a lot. I will talk with you soon."

You are out of there! Never stay and review the brochure and the video with them.

The 3-Way Teleconference Follow-Up

The Purpose: The objective of this 3-way call is to activate the "Greed" and "Curiosity" buttons of the new prospect to intrigue them to attend the BOP and sign-up with HGI.

The first thing a new recruit has is a believability problem with their friends and associates. The prospect brings the "trust factor" and the upline Leader brings the "believability factor."

The Upline Leader calls the new prospect and says:

"Hello _____ (new prospect), this is _____ (Leader). I'm a _____ (leader's title) with Hegemon Group International and I'm working with_____ (new Associate), who is one of our top up and coming leaders in the area. When I asked_____ (new Associate) who were some of the most ambitious people he/she knew, your name was on the top of the list. I know _____ (new Associate) gave you one of our brochures and videos. Did you get a chance to look at them?"

If they say, "NO, I haven't looked at it yet," the Upline Leader then says:

"No problem, but this company is attracting a lot of attention and the brochures and VIDEOs are in great demand. I need to send _____ (new Associate) by to pick them up by tomorrow. I encourage you to look through the brochure and watch the video before _____ (new Associate) comes by. Then you can decide if this is the right opportunity for you."

If they say, "YES, I've looked at it," without hesitation, the Upline Leader then says:

"Great, _____ (new Associate) and I are really excited about this. HGI is doing fabulous things to help people, and has the greatest income potential of any opportunity I have ever seen. You're not going to believe what a dynamic team _____ (new Associate) is building. At the pace he/she is going, he/she should be earning a second income of more than $100,000 in the next six months. _____ (new Associate) is here with me now and wants to say hello."

Recruit then says:

"_____ new prospect), I have never seen anything like this. The income potential here is truly amazing, and you know if I can do it, you can do it. I'm going to give you back to _____ (leader). What a great leader he/she is. _____ (Leader) is living proof that this business really works.

Upline then says:

"_____ (new prospect), I'm sure you want to learn how to double or triple your income over the next few months. You'll need to rearrange your schedule to give an hour or so to check this out – on either this Tuesday or Thursday night at 7:30. Which of those two nights is best for you?" (wait for answer) "Great _____ (new Associate) will come by your home around _:___ to pick you up or you can just follow him/her to the office. I look forward to seeing you _____ night."

If they say, "YES" with hesitation or if they resist, the Upline Leader then says:

"_____ (new prospect) I know you're busy just like everybody else, but I can tell you are the type of person who wants to make a lot more money while increasing your quality of life. Am I right?"

If they say, "YES" go back to the script.

If they say, "NO," then the Upline Leader says:

"I understand _____ (new prospect). _____ (new Associate) and I have some other calls to make, but we would love to get with you if your circumstances change. Worst case, we need to get with you to show you some of our consumer-oriented concepts and products that could save you and your family thousands of dollars without asking for any new money."

(Go ahead and schedule a time for a financial needs-analysis (FNA) appointment with your field builder.)

The key is to put your upline leader to work helping you follow-up with your Brochure/video drops to maximize your results.

VIDEO MOVEMENT/CIRCULATION REPORT

NAME _____   WEEK OF _____

No. of brochures purchased this week _____

No. of brochures/video links placed this week _____

No. of brochures picked up this week _____

No. of new associates recruited this week _____

No. of Product Presentations _____

No. of sales this week _____

	Prospect Name	Telephone Number	Date Placed	Date of Phone Follow-Up	Date Attended BOP	Date Brochures Picked Up	Match-Up Field Builder	Date Recruited	Data	Business Value on Sale
1										
2										
3										
4										
5										
6										
7										
8										
9										
10										
11										
12										
13										
14										
15										
16										
17										
18										
19										
20										

There are numerous methods you can use in the Approach/Contact phase. One of the most effective methods has always been the one-on-one phone invitation.

The Invitation Script

Be positive.	"Hi_____, this is _____." (brief small talk) "_____, I'm involved with an exciting new company that is doing some revolutionary things in the financial and real estate industry. You really need to take a look at this..."
1. Market the opportunity.	"This business is giving me a chance to do many of the things I've always dreamed of doing, such as..." (use four to five of your goals and dreams here) • start making my dreams come true • get paid what I'm really worth • start calling my own shots • build a second-income business • make a BIG career and lifestyle change • become debt free • save some serious money • have an option on whether or not my spouse needs to work • build my family's dream home • take control of my income and business life once and for all • be involved in a business that truly helps other people • _____ (don't pause here ... go on to the following:)
2. Get their attention. You are serious.	"But_____, I've never really had the chance to talk to you about these kinds of things. Would any of these be important to you?" [Wait for Answer (WFA) e.g. "Sure, but what is it?"] "_____, I don't have time to get too far into this over the phone right now, but you really need to see this opportunity." (WFA, usually yes)
3. Don't start answering questions.	"The name of the company is Hegemon Group International. It's a new marketing company just beginning its expansion here in the area, and it has tremendous income potential. I'm not going to try to explain it all to you now for a couple of reasons:
4. Explain why & stay in control.	• "I've just gotten started, and I don't know how to explain it all. You need to hear it from an expert." • "It takes about an hour to give a complete overview and I don't have an hour right now." • "There are some things you have to see visually for it to make sense, and we obviously can't do that over the phone."
5. Nail down the date.	"We're overviewing the company's business plan on _____, and again on _____. Which of those times would be best for you?" (Be firm, be positive, wait for answer.)
6. No decisions will be asked for that night.	"By the way, the purpose of the presentation is simply to provide people with an introduction to the company. If you want to look into it further, there will be more information about the company available at the end of the presentation for you to review. No one will be asking you to make a decision about it at that time ... Fair enough?" (WFA)
7. Pick them up.	"_____, this will also give us a chance to spend some time together. I'll pick you up, and you can tell me what you think on the way home." (SAY THANK YOU AND HANG UP!!!! YOU ARE DONE.)

Overcoming Objections in the Invitation Script

Occasionally in the course of invitation script, the prospect may begin to ask questions such as:

"What is it?"
"What are you selling?"
"Before I come, I'd like to know more."

To avoid the Scenario of Disaster and maintain the integrity of the invitation, you will need a few choice responses to regain control of the conversation. Here is an example of how it could go:

Prospect:	"Before I commit to coming to a meeting, what is it?"
You:	"Well_____, as I told you, I am really not the one to explain this to you, and it does take a good hour to do it justice. The purpose of the meeting is simply to provide you with an introduction to the company. If you want to look into it further, there will be some literature and information for you to take home. No one will be asking you to make a decision at that time. Fair enough?" (WFA)
You:	"So, will Tuesday or Thursday night be better?"

If he/she still resists:

Prospect:	"I would really like to know more."
You:	"Let me ask you a question. When I asked you earlier if you wanted to hear about a serious, legitimate opportunity and you said, 'Yes,' were you serious?"

If "NO" (I was not serious)

"Thanks, if you ever change your mind, feel free to give me a call."

If "YES" (I was serious)

"Great. Now, is Tuesday or Thursday night better?"

If he/she still resists:

Prospect:	"I really don't want to come to any meeting without knowing more about it."
You:	"I appreciate that, but it's real important that you hear about this business. Tell you what I will do. I'll get one of my senior Leaders and we will come by your home and tell you about the company. Is Monday or Wednesday better?"

Overcoming Objections in the Invitation Script *(continued)*

If he/she still resists:

Prospect: " I'm not coming to any meeting nor is anyone coming to my house until you tell me more."
(Usually never gets this far)

You: " I appreciate how you feel, but I'm not going to mess this up for you. Here's my number
_____-_____. You give me a call when you feel like attending a meeting, but don't
put it off too long - this is a once-in-a-lifetime company, and I know it could be the
chance of a lifetime for us! Talk to you soon. Bye."

Whoever blinks first loses. Odds are if it did get this far, by you not answering his questions, his curiosity is
still piqued and he will most likely call you down the road. Or if not, the timing was wrong, and it would have
been a waste of your time anyway.

For training and educational purposes only. Not to be used with the public.

38

Hubert Humphrey's Proven Field-Tested Secrets For Overcoming Objections

During Hubert's field era, he absolutely mastered the art of talking to people. He knew exactly how to respond to any given situation. You can do the same by following his field-tested secrets.

When prospects start asking questions, here are the basic responses:

"What difference does it make?   When did you get so picky?"

"What do you want it to be?"

Prospect:	"Is it sales?"
You:	"Do you want it to be?"
Prospect:	"No."
You:	"Great, you're going to love this."
Prospect:	"Yes."
You:	"Great, you're going to love this."

Basically, you give the same answer no matter what they say, and just play along with them.

The key is to take charge, know what they're going to say, and overcome it.

This is also your opportunity to hit two of your prospect's buttons:

1. Greed Button - Let your prospect know there is big money to be made here.
2. Curiosity Button - Withhold information until you're ready to give it.

The Invitation

Calling for a New Teammate:

"_____ (Target Market Name), this is _____ (Your Name), how are you? I'm calling because we have a mutual friend in _____ (New Name), and he/she recently joined our firm. While we were reviewing his/her business plan, your name was mentioned. I promised I'd give you a call today, so we could run a business idea by you. Okay?"

Calling for an Existing Teammate:

"_____ (Target Market Name), this is _____ (Your Name), how are you? I'm calling because we have a mutual friend in _____ (New Name), and he/she and I are in business together. Recently, while we were reviewing his/her business plan, your name was mentioned. I promised I'd give you a call today, so we could run a business idea by you. Okay?"

Calling with a Teammate:

"_____ (Referral), this is _____ (Trainer). I am on the phone with _____ (Associate) and he/she recently joined our firm. Say hi, _____ (Teammate). (Establish friendly link and new associate edifies trainer.) Recently while we were reviewing his/her business plan, your name was mentioned. I promised I'd give you a call today so we could run a business idea by you. Okay?"

Invitation Script Follow-Up:

1. Invite a prospect or client. (Include spouses, refer to invitation tracts.)

2. Call your leader and tell him/her that you have someone coming to the meeting and give him/her their name and occupation.

3. One to two days before the meeting, follow up with a phone call to confirm the guest's attendance.

   Tell him/her:

   " Hi_____ this is _____ with Hegemon Group International. I'm calling to confirm our getting together tomorrow night for tech meeting and also, to let you know that you can bring interested contacts with you if you desire. I have told my Marketing Director that you are coming. He is looking forward to meeting you and has reserved special seats for you and your spouse.

   " I'm excited about getting together with you. I'll pick you up at 6:30 P.M. (or 9:00 A.M. for Saturday morning meetings). Remember, you'll want to dress for a business meeting."

For training and educational purposes only. Not to be used with the public.

40

Step 3   The Presentation

Business Opportunity Presentation

Purpose: To Sell the dream.

THE PRESENTATION

There is no meeting more important than your next Business Opportunity Presentation (BOP).

The main purposes of a BOP:

1. Resell the dream to your existing Leaders.
2. Teach existing Leaders how to sell the dream.
3. Sell the dream to new prospects and set a follow-up Get Started Interview in the next one or two days.

Before you see what actually happens in the BOP itself, it's time to take a deeper look at the dynamics of a successful meeting.

Create "The Mozone" - running the Dream-Selling Machine and creating an exciting, quality, professional recruiting environment. Capitalize on the magic of crowds, the synergy that is created by large groups of people.

The more people you have, the greater sense of urgency to get in and get started. The excitement and enthusiasm become contagious. The success of your meetings will be dictated by the size of your crowds. With Hegemon Group International, you have so much to work with, it's nearly impossible to give a "bad" presentation.

- **The BOP**
  The psychology of the BOP has proven to be highly successful. All you have to do is learn how to master it.

- **The One-on-One BOP**
  The second option is the one-on-one BOP. Focus on how to make a powerful one-on-one presentation.

- **The HOP**
  The third option is the HOP. The Home Opportunity Presentation provides an intimate atmosphere for friends, family and colleagues.

Creating MoZone at the BOP:

(MoZone = Momentum Zone)

1. **Be prepared mentally.**

   Your enthusiasm, conviction, and team spirit will have a tremendous influence on the impression we make.

2. **Remember, people respond based on what they feel more than what they hear.**

   Studies have shown that what is really communicated to people is based on the following:
   - 7% content (verbal)
   - 38% tone of voice
   - 55% body language

   We are not just attracting people to a business, we are going to attract them to our **environment**! The atmosphere of the office at the BOP or at any training session is crucial to a successful recruiting meeting. Arrive at least 30 minutes before the Business Opportunity Presentation begins so that you and your guests can help create and benefit from the "MoZone." Have HGI banners, posters, awards and uplifting music to create the proper atmosphere in your meeting room.

3. **Make sure to have a professional appearance.**

   You must be dressed for a business meeting. Proper business attire (coat and tie for men and appropriate business attire for women) is to be worn by all guests and team members.

4. **When you arrive, go directly into the Business Opportunity meeting room.**

   Circulate and help create a friendly atmosphere. Make sure you personally greet each guest. Stay in the meeting room until after the announcements have been made and you are dismissed for classes, etc...

   1) **Do not** hang around in the halls, lobby, sidewalk, parking lot, etc... If you are waiting for a guest, wait in the Business Opportunity meeting room only.

   2) **Do not** neutralize the excitement of the environment with technical details or negatives.

5. **Have ALL guests sign the register, and get a name tag.**

   (Use standard name badges - red for new guests, blue for existing associates.)

Creating MoZone at the BOP *(continued)*

6. **Properly use "Leadership Edification."**

    Introduce your guest(s) to your leaders and the speaker. This helps develop a closeness between the speaker and your guest(s). Make sure to use your guest's name often during conversation with the speaker to insure the name will be remembered through association, and used in interaction during the meeting. Remember, the use of a person's name is a positive form of recognition.

7. **Find your guest(s) a seat near the front.**

    Fill in existing seats before requesting new ones to be set up. There will be a chair monitor; you and your guests don't set up chairs! Do not sit with your guest(s) unless you are staying for the entire meeting.

8. **If you're not going to be staying in the meeting with your guest(s)...**

    Tell them that while they're spending time with _____, you will be in the next room in the training class and that you will meet them as soon as the meeting is over, and to enjoy their time with _____.

9. **If you're going to be staying in the meeting with your guest(s)...**

    1) **Do not** talk during the meeting.
    2) **Do not** answer questions the speaker asks the crowd during the meeting.
    3) **Do not** get up and leave during the meeting.
    4) **Remember,** before and after the meeting is for the **guests**. If you have any questions, comments or things you need to take care of, wait until **all** of the **guests** are gone.

10. **Toward the end of the meeting, RMDs and other Leaders will be introduced.**

    People who hold these positions have earned the right to be introduced individually and these Leaders typically will be setting the Get Started interview.

11. **When the meeting ends, hand out the presentation questionnaires.**

    Make sure to collect all the forms once the guests have filled them out.

While the meeting is in session:

It is imperative that any conversation or business conducted in the lobby or halls be done very quietly so as not to disturb or distract those in the meeting! Also, never re-enter the meeting once it is in session. Late guests must be handled one-on-one.

The BOP Flow

Now that everyone knows their role and their assignment, it's show time:

- MoZone begins promptly 30 minutes prior to the meeting. All Leaders should be in meeting room with their guests meeting the other new guests and using Leadership edification.

- Meeting should always begin on time with all attendees in main meeting room.

- The person starting the meeting should always:

    − Welcome the crowd.
    − Put them at ease.
    − Remind people to turn off their cell phones.
    − Ask people to hold their questions until the end.
    − Edify the BOP presenter and give them a proper introduction.

- After introduction and announcements, new guests will remain in meeting room and newer associates will quickly and quietly follow instructors to the appropriate class.

- Five minutes prior to the end of BOP, all instructors and class attendees should return to the main meeting room for the last part of BOP and to be in place to set follow-up interviews with invited guests.

The BOP Presentation

To make the most effective presentation possible, you must operate with the proper marketing tools.

- Use a notebook or tablet PC connected to a large flat screen monitor or projector.

- Always use the HGI official presentation (BOP flipchart) available in the back office.

- When presenting one-on-one or very small groups, use a notebook screen with a 13"-17" display or the official HGI BOP flipchart presentation booklet.

- Using an HGI Recruiting Video available at HGIPlay.com is optional but powerful.

- These BOP presentations have proven to work in our largest markets. Watch the weekly BOP webinars, access transcripts of HGI leaders' BOP presentations at HGIUniversity.com. Become an effective BOP presenter and train the leaders on your team to do the same.

For training and educational purposes only. Not to be used with the public.

44

Subliminal Messages of a BOP

Master these and become a master builder. These are the things that will set you apart.

1. Keep the meeting simple, never complicated.

2. Have a conversational style, with an easy and pleasant delivery. Your presentation should be solid, but not flashy. Ideally, you will give a one-on-one delivery to the group.

3. Show the big income potential - people want to know that they have the opportunity to make a large income.

4. Solidify the company by talking about our preferred companies and the administrative support.

5. Build around these main points:
   - You can do it.
   - There's big money to be made here.
   - These are good people doing good things to help people.

6. Dreams can come true. People from all walks of life have become successful and so can you.

7. Keep an exciting, fun pace - make people feel good.

8. Send the message loud and clear - it's the ground floor and it's time to start today.

9. Talk about the importance of families as you sell the dream.

10. Make people feel good - make them feel special. Make the extra effort to call people by their names from the stage. Make them feel as if they're part of the meeting.

HGI MoZone Music Suggestions

Walk-in and walk-out music is a huge part of any successful HGI Meeting. The music selections below are in no set order. They are mixed, interchangeable and substituted based on crowd response, time of day, size of audience, etc. While no one particular formula exists for the MoZone Music which will best stimulate your BOP or meeting, the following titles (more than two hours of music) have brought about positive results.

Getting Better, Get Back & Revolution – The Beatles
Centerfield – John Fogerty
Start Me Up – The Rolling Stones
House Is A Rockin' – Stevie Ray Vaughn
Soak Up The Sun – Cheryl Crow
Running Down The Dream, American Girl – Tom Petty
Don't Stop Thinking About Tomorrow – Fleetwood Mac
Livin' In The USA – Steve Miller Band
Living In America – James Brown
Right Here, Right Now, Jump – Van Halen
Simply The Best – Tina Turner
What I Like About You – The Romantics
Rock And Roll All Night, Detroit Rock City – KISS
Freedom, Jet, Live and Let Die – Paul McCartney
We Can Be Heroes – Traveling Wilburys
Everybody Have Fun Tonight – Wang Chung

Instant Karma – John Lennon
Glory Days, Dancing In The Dark – Bruce Springsteen
Shining Star & Let's Grove – Earth Wind & Fire
Mr. Blue Sky, Tight Rope – ELO
Soul Man – The Blues Brothers
Eye of the Tiger – Rocky IV Soundtrack
River of Dreams, We Didn't Start the Fire – Billy Joel
R.O.C.K. In the USA – John Mellancamp
Hit Me With Your Best Shot – Pat Benatar
Celebration – Kool & The Gang
I'm So Excited, Neutron Dance – The Pointer Sisters
Freeze Frame – J. Geils Band
Working for a Living, Power of Love & Heart of Rock N Roll –
Huey Lewis and The News
Greatest Sports Rock & Jams – ESPN Jock Rock
Vertigo, Beautiful Day – U2

It is also important to note that to play music like this at your meetings; you must pay royalties and licensing fees. For information regarding these fees, contact BMI, Inc. 10 Music Square East, Nashville, TN 37203-4310 or call 1-800-925-8451. All licensing information should be listed with your name, not Hegemon Group International.

The Role of the BOP Presenter

- The BOP Presenter should be your most dynamic, most enthusiastic, strongest Leader in the center with a current track record of success.

- The BOP Presenter should study and master the BOP training at HGIUniversity.com or other company training materials to learn how to give a winning presentation.

- The BOP Presenter should not rotate - it should always be your best Leader.

- The BOP Presenter must have a "closer's mentality" to help move the prospect to a recruit decision.

- If your best presenter feels that he/she can't put forth his/her best effort on a given night, replace them with the next best presenter.

- This is not a place to practice. People work too hard to bring guests to the BOP. Let presenters practice at home with their families.

- Keep all negatives away from presenter before the BOP. The presenter must be excited.

After the Meeting

1. People really do want to be led and supported.

2. Take your new guest(s) to get a BOP decision kit, and always avoid the "Scenario of Disaster."

3. After picking up the kit, take your guest(s) to your Leader to set up an appointment for a follow-up interview. If he/she resists, stay in control and take him/her to meet your Leader.

4. When setting the appointment, be supportive of the person making the appointment.

   If your guest(s) needs to reschedule his/her appointment, tell him/her to call the person with whom he/she set the appointment and to do so as soon as possible.

5. It's important that all of these steps (the first three Speed Filters) take place within 10 to 15 minutes.

6. Make sure all guests complete the BOP questionnaire before they leave and turn it in to the upline Leader.

7. Time is of the essence. The recruit will never be more excited than when they leave the meeting. The first 24 to 48 hours demand the full attention of both you and your Leader.

The BOP Decision Kit

You should prepare BOP decision kits for your guests in advance. These kits can be sold at cost (typically $10) and should include the current approved versions of our best recruiting materials.

For training and educational purposes only. Not to be used with the public.

46

The Meeting after the Meeting

Once all the appointments have been set with the new guests, it's time for the meeting after the meeting.

- This is your chance to have a weekly huddle with your Leaders.

- Recognize new team members and introduce them to the team.

- Build relationships among the entire team.

- Fight the war of focus - help the team stay focused.

- Discuss the current month's goals and re-sell the vision.

- Identify potential Leaders and rising superstars.

- The main objective is to determine the goal for the current week, and share responsibility with team Leaders.

- Each team member leaves the meeting knowing his/her responsibility for the week.

Key Areas of Focus in the BOP

- Monitor the number of people - "old" and "new" - you have at BOPs. Use the BOP Possibility Projection sheet and the BOP Attendance Log.

- The average number of people per month at your BOPs = the average number of sales per month in your base shop.

- "Where performance is measured, performance improves."

One-on-One/Home BOPs

1. **One-on-One BOPs (BOP = Business Opportunity Presentation)**

   WHAT? When you can't get the prospect to a big BOP night, take it to them
   (use the current Leaders With Vision flip chart).

   WHERE? Home, office, restaurant, work, where two or more are gathered.

   WHEN? Breakfast time, mid-morning, lunchtime, afternoons, dinnertime, evenings
   (anytime and all-the-time).

        4 to 5 days/nights per week.

   WHO? Friends, neighbors, relatives, co-workers, social contacts, business associates
   (anybody and everybody).

   HOW? With enthusiasm and emotion.
   Speed width/speed depth.
   Feed into group BOPs.

2. **Home BOPs (HOP = Home Opportunity Presentation)**

   - The current HGI BOP presentation

   - Three to 10 key couples

   - BOP Decision Kit/HGI Products and Services handout/Video Link Invitations (hgiplay.com)

   - Enthusiasm about opportunity

   - Feed into group BOPs

   - Two to three per week

For training and educational purposes only. Not to be used with the public.

48

HGI
HEGEMON GROUP INTERNATIONAL

POSSIBILITY PROJECTIONS FOR INVITEES

Business Opportunity Presentation Leader: _____

Location: _____

Business Opportunity Presentation Date: _____

	Name	Invitee's Name	Phone	New or Active	Upline	Committed to Attend
1						
2						
3						
4						
5						
6						
7						
8						
9						
10						
11						
12						
13						
14						
15						
16						
17						
18						
19						
20						
21						
22						
23						
24						
25						

(Includes New Prospects & Existing Team Members Contacted & Committed to Attend)

BOP Leadership Assignments

BOP Location_____

Date	Chair Monitor	MoZone/AV	Greeters	BOP Sign-In Sheet	Name Badges	Emcee	BOP Presenter(s)	Fast Start Class	Training Class #____	Training Class #____	Sell Kits

Write names in each box that applies for each Leader's assignments.

BOP ATTENDANCE LOG

Date	Site

Name	Address (City, State, Zip)	Phone Number	Who invited You?	1st Meeting Yes/No?	Leader	Follow-Up Interview (RMD will set date)

HEGEMON GROUP INTERNATIONAL

PRESENTATION QUESTIONNAIRE

Name:	Cell Phone:
Business Phone:	E-mail:
Address:	Facebook:
City, State, Zip:	Twitter:
Who invited you?	Upline RMD:

Decisions/Objectives:

I am interested in:

THE BUSINESS

☐ I want to begin building a second income.

☐ I am ready to sign up to get started now.

☐ I want to begin _____ evenings per week.

THE CONCEPTS AND PRODUCTS

☐ I am interested in building financial security for my family.

☐ I am interested in having a full financial services product review.

☐ I am interested in having my mortgage loan evaluated.

☐ I am planning on buying or selling a home in the next several months.

☐ I am interested in having a financial needs analysis done on my 401(k) plan and/or other investments.

☐ I want to learn how to save more money.

COMMENTS:

_____

_____

_____

_____

_____

PLEASE RETURN BEFORE LEAVING

Step 4 | *The Follow-Up*

Mastering the Art of the Follow-Up

Purpose: To move the prospect through Filters 1-4 of the Eight Speed Filters.

THE FOLLOW-UP

Just as important as controlling the point of contact on the front-end, the follow-up is equally critical on the back-end. The objective of the follow-up is always to move the prospect through the first four Speed Filters as quickly as possible.

The filters do exactly what they say. They filter out the people who are not serious about the opportunity, and allow you to focus on the ones who are. You can tell a person's commitment level by how far and how fast they move through the Eight Speed Filters.

When the follow-up is properly executed, you will help save people from themselves and you will recruit a higher percentage of people. At the same time, you will have a higher volume of production - a by-product of running the system.

The Follow-Up Process (Speed Filters No. 1 - 4)

1. Stay After the Meeting.
2. Get a Decision Kit.
3. Set a Get Started Interview.
4. Keep the Appointment and Sign Up.

(Filters No. 5 - 8 will be covered in Step 5 – The Start-Up.)

The LFS Eight Speed Filters

The Speed Filters are the best way to keep a new recruit on track for success, and are the ultimate indicators of interest.

Speed Filters 1-4 — Step 4: The Follow-Up
Filter No. 1 – Stay After the Meeting.

If your guest doesn't want to hurry out the door, and wants to stay after the meeting, this is your first sign that you have a potential hot new recruit.

When the meeting ends, go directly to your guest(s), set a positive mood, and say: "Wasn't that great? Here is a copy of our products and services overview, now let's get a decision kit." Don't ask them what they think, or ask them any other questions.

If they agree: Take your guest(s) to get a kit, then meet with your Leader to set up an appointment for a Get Started Interview. If they resist, or don't want to buy a kit, say: "Ok, but I promised _____ that we'd say good night before we left." Stay in control, and turn and walk toward your Leader. When you get there, say, "_____ wanted to say goodbye."

The Leader then says, "It was great having you here. Did you get a kit?" (WFA) When the prospect says "no," the leader then says, "why not?" (in a very polite manner). This question gives the experienced Leader the opportunity to identify and overcome any objections and/or questions that the prospect has that has caused them not to get a kit. Worse case, if the prospect decides they don't want to join, the Leader can then set an appointment to review their data to determine which of our products are best for them.

Filter No. 2 – Get a Decision Kit.

If your new recruit buys a decision kit, you know they are serious about learning more about the opportunity.

The reason we "sell" the kit to the new prospects instead of giving it to them is because everyone will take something if it's free. It would then be impossible to determine their level of seriousness.

The Leader will review the kit and explain why it costs $5 or $10. The kit should include the following items in one envelope:

• Promo flyer for link to HGI videos (hgiplay.com)
• "The Play" brochure
• "How To Win The Money Game"
• "Leverage the Winds of Fortune" brochure
• Getting Started Check List and Fast Start Check List

Brochures can be purchased at the HGISuccessStore.com.
Printable PDFs are available at HGIUniversity.com

Filter No. 3 – Set a Get Started Interview.

Setting a time to attend a Get Started interview is the next filter in determining the commitment level of your new guest.

When setting the appointment, be supportive to the person making the appointment. Let the Leader handle any objections the guest might have.

If your guest(s) need to reschedule his/her appointment, tell them to call the person with whom they set the appointment, and to do so as soon as possible. Once you find out a need for rescheduling, immediately call your Leader and let him know your guest will be calling to reschedule.

Filter No. 4 – Keep the Appointment and Sign Up.

This is the last, and most important, filter in step 4 - The Follow-Up. When a new prospect returns for the Get Started Interview and joins the company, it is the sign of a major commitment from a person who is very serious about the business.

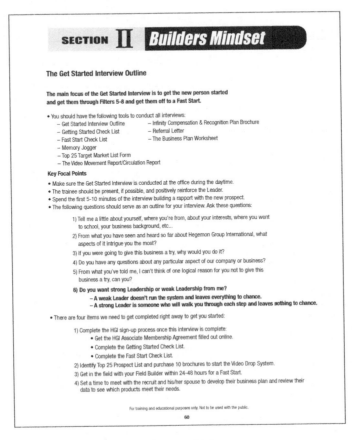

(See page 60.)

For training and educational purposes only. Not to be used with the public.

Notes:

Step 5 | The Start-Up

The Fast Start Challenge

Purpose: The Get Started Interview is a systematic way to get the new recruit off to a fast start by completing Filters 5-8 of the Eight Speed Filters.

THE START-UP

Just as the first few days of an infant's life are critical to his/her health and well-being, the first few days for a new recruit set the tone for his/her business career.

While all the components of the start-up are important, nothing is more critical than beginning to build the recruit's business by surrounding him/her with new recruits. You must instill in the new recruit a 100 percent commitment to growth from day one.

1. The Start-Up Process (Speed Filters No. 5 - 8)

- Develop a Prospect List.
- Set Goals/Create Business Plan.
- Do Financial Needs Analysis (FNA) Internal Consumption as needed.
- Match-Up with Field Builder to Qualify for Associate Promotion.

2. Field Building

Field Building is a very important area of focus and activity in your business. To succeed, you must become a field-building expert and establish the prototype for your teammates to duplicate.

3. The Magic of the Match-Up System

The Match-Up System is the key to your ability to continue to get wide with new direct leaders.

4. How to Build a Big Base Shop

The future of HGI belongs to those who build big Base Shops.

5. The Sales Process

Remember, every presentation is a recruiting presentation. Always sell HGI's concepts first, and close every presentation by asking for referrals.

Speed Filters 5-8 — Step 5: The Start-Up

Filter No. 5 – Develop a Prospect List.

When a new recruit is willing to create a prospect list, you know they are excited about our opportunity and they're willing to share it with people they know.

- Start one on the spot and you as the Leader, lead the way. Have the spouse participate when possible.

- Qualify Top 25 for a Fast Start.

- Teach new recruit how to become a master inviter and review the Scenario of Disaster.

- Use the 3-part Top 25 prospect list forms. You keep a copy of the Prospect List to help track and monitor the new recruit's progress. The other copy goes to the upline RMD.

- Also, to maximize the new recruit's influence, make sure to get them to sign 25 referral letters.

(See LFS Manual, page 18.)

Filter No. 6 – Set Goals/Create Business Plan.

When the new recruit shares his dreams with you and sets goals to accomplish them, you know they are starting on the path to success. Review the components of a Winning Business Plan and their Business Plan worksheet to help them get started.

(See LFS Manual, page 64.)

Filter No. 7 – Do Financial Needs Analysis (FNA) / Internal Consumption as Needed.

One of the strongest indications of a person's commitment is when they take action and begin to build their team.

1. Assign a Field Builder to every new recruit immediately.

2. The Field Builder controls the point of contact as the new recruit uses the video drop system to get new prospects to the next BOP. The new recruit should buy 10 brochures and circulate them at least two and a half times, which should result in 10-15 presentations.

3. The Field Builder holds one-on-one BOPs with the new recruit (for those who don't attend a group BOP).

4. The Field Builder conducts Get Started interviews.

5. The Field Builder helps them make their field training sales. Refer to the Field Building section on page 77 of the LFS Manual for more details.

6. Make sure each new recruit immediately signs up with HGI to ensure that they are quality recruits.

7. Qualify for the Fast Start Award with 5 new quality personal recruits and 5 qualified field training sales in the first 30 days.

Filter No. 8 – Match-Up with Field Builder to Qualify for Associate Promotion.

When a new recruit completes their personal data, you know you have a committed recruit who believes in what we do for people. It's tough to commit others to something that you yourself don't practice.

• Leader reviews the data for new associate and spouse and helps them determine which concepts and products fit their individual needs.

(See LFS Manual, page 91.)

The Get Started Interview Outline

The main focus of the Get Started Interview is to get the new person started and get them through Filters 5-8 and get them off to a Fast Start.

- You should have the following tools to conduct all interviews:
  - Get Started Interview Outline
  - Getting Started Check List
  - Fast Start Check List
  - Memory Jogger
  - Top 25 Target Market List Form
  - The Video Movement Report/Circulation Report
  - Infinity Compensation & Recognition Plan Brochure
  - Referral Letter
  - The Business Plan Worksheet

Key Focal Points

- Make sure the Get Started Interview is conducted at the office during the daytime.
- The trainee should be present, if possible, and positively reinforce the Leader.
- Spend the first 5-10 minutes of the interview building a rapport with the new prospect.
- The following questions should serve as an outline for your interview. Ask these questions:

  1) Tell me a little about yourself, where you're from, about your interests, where you went to school, your business background, etc...

  2) From what you have seen and heard so far about Hegemon Group International, what aspects of it intrigue you the most?

  3) If you were going to give this business a try, why would you do it?

  4) Do you have any questions about any particular aspect of our company or business?

  5) From what you've told me, I can't think of one logical reason for you not to give this business a try, can you?

  6) Do you want strong Leadership or weak Leadership from me?

      – A weak Leader doesn't run the system and leaves everything to chance.
      – A strong Leader is someone who will walk you through each step and leaves nothing to chance.

- There are four items we need to get completed right away to get you started:

  1) Complete the HGI sign-up process once this interview is complete:
     - Get the HGI Associate Membership Agreement filled out online.
     - Complete the Getting Started Check List.
     - Complete the Fast Start Check List.

  2) Identify Top 25 Prospect List and purchase 10 brochures to start the Video Drop System.

  3) Get in the field with your Field Builder within 24-48 hours for a Fast Start.

  4) Set a time to meet with the recruit and his/her spouse to develop their business plan and review their data to see which products meet their needs.

Getting Started Check List

Success demands that you complete this entire Check List to maximize the HGI opportunity.

☐ **Join Hegemon Group International:**
— Use your Sponsor's link to complete the sign-up process at HGICrusade.com. Choose either the Gold or Silver Plan. Receive your HGI Member ID and make a note of it.
— Pay your HGI membership and technology fees.* Non-refundable.
— Receive your HGI Member ID and make note of it.

☐ **Review the Features and Links in Your Back Office:**
— Follow all instructions in the "Getting Started Section" of your HGICrusade.com back office.

☐ **Review Product Provider Resources in your HGICrusade.com Back Office:**
— Review Licensed Products under the Innovation Partners and HFG Sections.
— Review the Non-Licensed Products section.

☐ **Getting Licensed:**
— Review the Licensing Resources in your HGICrusade.com back office.

☐ **Complete the HGI Required Documents:**
— Reference the "Required Documents" link under Resources in the HGICrusade.com back office.
— Follow the instructions listed in this section on how to submit your completed forms.

☐ **Complete Your Fast Start Check List**

For training and educational purposes only. Not to be used with the public.

61

Fast Start Check List

Success demands urgent completion of this entire Check List to maximize the HGI opportunity.

☐ **Complete Getting Started Check List**

☐ **Prospecting - Create A Target Market List**
— Begin to develop your prospect list with a goal of a minimum of 100 names.
— Use the Executive Memory Jogger to add as many names as possible to your list.
— Identify the "Top 10/25" on your list and get 10 videos dropped in the first week.
  (If your car broke down in the middle of the night, who would you call?)

☐ **The Approach/Contact**
— Control the point of contact.
— Avoid the scenario of disaster.
  Your enthusiasm creates curiosity. They ask questions. You attempt to answer questions.
  You answer wrong!!! (From incorrect or incomplete information.) They jump to conclusions. The result is failure!!!
— Match-Up with your Field Builder and begin running the Video Drop System/"The Play"

☐ **Order Your Marketing Tools**

— Login to HGICrusade.com and be sure your Gold or Silver package is activated to be eligible to earn commissions and full overrides on all product sales from you and your team.
— Visit www.HGISuccessStore.com and order all of your supplies:
  - Business Cards
  - Video Drop System Materials:
    • Decision Kit Materials: (5 each of: *How to Win the Money Game*, *The Play*, *Leverage the Winds of Fortune*)
    •10 Copies of the *Secrets of Money*
  - Reference materials:
    • Leadership Format System Manual
    • Unlocking the Secrets of the System Book (5 copies)
    • Magic of Compound Recruiting Book
  - Recommended items to download and print:
    • 10 copies of the Video Link Invitation
    • 20 copies of HGI Products and Services Brochure
    • HGI All-the-Forms Document (print individual pages as needed)

☐ **Plan To Attend Upcoming Company Events**
— Next Local Meeting: _____ Date: _____
— Next Company Big Event: _____ Date: _____
— Other Upcoming Events: _____ Date: _____

☐ **The Presentation – BOP & One-on-One** _____
— Get your prospects to the next meeting - or take the meeting to them one-on-one.
— Commit to attend all weekly BOP meetings and company events for ongoing training and motivation.
— Dress for all BOP meetings is business - coat and tie for men and business attire for women.

☐ **Complete Your Personal Data**
— Review all of our products and services for your personal needs.

☐ **Start Training Process With Certified Field Builder**
— Field Builder assigned by upline RMD.
— Match-Up with your Field Builder for a Fast Start to Quality Associate.
— Fast Start Award - 5 personal recruits and 5 qualified Field Training sales in first 30 days.

☐ **Set An Appointment With Your Leader Within the First 24-48 Hours**
— Discuss your product and service needs.
— Make sure your spouse is recruited and committed to the business.
— Finish your prospect list and any other paperwork.

The 6 Components of A Great Business Plan

A winning business plan helps to develop a clear concise plan of action to guide your activity and dramatically improve your level of performance.

The greatest example of Goal Setting and Business Plan Development is Napoleon Hill's all-time motivational book, *Think & Grow Rich*. Study closely the section titled: " *Six ways to Turn Your Desires into Gold.*"

1. Fix in your mind the exact amount of new associates, sales, promotions, income, etc. you desire. It is not sufficient merely to say, "I want plenty of new associates, sales, promotions, income." Be definite as to the amount! There is a psychological reason for definiteness.

2. Determine exactly what you intend to give in return, to achieve the goals and dreams you desire. There is no such reality as "something for nothing." You must be committed – "I will have at least five appointments this week, five BOP attendees, etc."

3. Establish a definite date when you intend to possess whatever goals you desire. Commit to your deadlines.

4. Create a definite plan for carrying out your desire and begin at once, whether you are ready or not, to put this plan into action.

5. Write out a clear, concise statement of the specific goals and objectives you intend to achieve, determine the time limit for their acquisition, state what you intend to give in return for the things you desire, and describe clearly the plan through which you intend to achieve your goals.

6. Read your written statement aloud, twice daily, once just before retiring at night, and once after waking up in the morning; as you read, see, feel and believe yourself already in possession of your goals and objectives. It is especially important that you observe and follow the instructions in this paragraph. You may complain that is impossible for you to "see yourself in possession of recruits and sales" (or whatever) before you actually have them. Here is where a burning desire will come to your aid. You must imagine how good it is going to feel when you achieve these goals.

Points to Remember:

1. Write deep and important emotions into your plan.

2. You must read good books to grow and be inspired. Supplement your reading with CDs from HGI Leaders and other quality speakers/teachers.

3. Control your associations. Nothing drains your energy faster than spending time with negative people.

4. Draw your inspiration and reward from building others.

5. Help/challenge others to achieve their own goals, not yours. They are certainly not in this business for you!

6. Have and keep high, positive expectations with standards of excellence.

HEGEMON GROUP INTERNATIONAL

The 6 Components of a Great Business Plan
"Your Plan to Turn Your Desires into Gold."

(You must complete this worksheet specifically and exactly to make your dreams come true.)

_____   _____

Current Level   Next Promotion Level

_____   _____

Current Production   Promotion Requirements

1) Exact amount of new associates_____, sales_____, points_____, income_____ you desire each month.

2) Exactly what you will give in return for this:

_____ Number of evenings/hours per week

_____ Number of brochure/video drops per week

_____ Number of BOP invitations per week

_____ Number of BOP attendees per week

_____ Number of Get Started interviews per week

_____ Number of new recruits per week

_____ Number of product presentations per week

_____ Number of new clients per week

3) Definite date when you will possess the recruits, sales, points and income: _____

4) Definite date when you will write out your clear, concise detailed
   statement and plan: _____

5) Definite date you will turn your plan into action: _____

6) Definite times each day when you will read aloud your written statement,
   while vividly imagining yourself in possession of the income and
   new associates: _____ a.m.

                                                          _____ p.m.

10 Keys to Get Your Career Off to a Fast Start:

The first few days of a new recruit's life are the most critical ones in their career. They have seen the potential of the HGI opportunity and are excited about the chance to build a tremendous future for their family. The key is to get on track from day one doing all the things that success demands.

HGI Road Map to Success

1. Commit to attend the local area Business Opportunity Meeting (BOP) weekly.

The BOP is the heart of the HGI Leadership Format System. It serves as your hub for recruiting, building and training. There is no meeting more important than the next BOP.

2. Learn Step 2 of the Leadership Format System (LFS) and begin inviting people to the next BOP.

You must master the Video Drop System and get 10 Brochures/Video Links out ASAP following the system. Your upline will gladly be of assistance in teaching you this most important part of the LFS.

3. Complete all of the Eight Speed Filters.

These Filters will help you start your business on the right track. Completing these steps in the fastest time possible also lets your leaders know how serious you are about the business.

4. Register for the next company big event.

You build your business from big event to big event. The HGI Convention of Champions in the summer and HGI Top Gun meeting in the fall, are critical in stretching your vision to new heights. Log in today to HGICrusade.com and register for the next big event.

5. Plug into the Production Format System.

Follow this simple step-by-step process to enhance the financial security for you, your family, and your teammates by taking advantage of the powerful HGI products and services (Internal consumption).

6. Get on HGI Text Network.

This network will tie you directly into the HGI information flow. This tool allows you to message your team as well as receive messages from your upline, the company and from Hubert Humphrey himself. You can text Hubert directly and get advice and training from the master builder himself. Log in to your HGI back office - click on dashboard, then click on "HGI Text Network".

For training and educational purposes only. Not to be used with the public.

65

HGI Road Map to Success continued

7. Sign up for either the IVO technology package (silver) or LFSMAX Technology Package (gold, recommended) .

Build your business 24/7 with your own HGI personalized marketing web pages. Learn about LFSMAX at LFSmax.com and inside HGIUniversity.com

8. Login to HGIUniversity.com and begin HGIU training for HGI and all product provider companies.

The HGI opportunity allows you to make commissions and overrides from some of the most exciting industries in business and sign up for all of HGI's preferred product providers and then complete all of the required training and certifications through HGI University.

9. Visit the HGICrusade.com website often for company news and information.

HGI has one of the most exciting websites in all of marketing. From the dynamic public site, to the many tools you will find in the associate login section, you will find this a valuable asset to help build your business.

10. Become a Qualified Associate.

Every new associate must immediately sign up with HGI and get assigned a Field Builder to complete all field training requirements and recruit at least one person to become "Qualified Associate" and be eligible for company contests, bonus pools and equity share.

Set Goals

30-Day Fast Start Challenge

The first 30 days are pivotal to your HGI career. You alone set standards of excellence that will carry on for all of your future HGI Leaders.

	(recruits/sales/days)
Slow Start	3/3/30
Average Start	4/4/30
Fast Start	**5/5/30 — Qualify for Fast Start Award**
Super Start	10/10/30

Challenge yourself to get off to a Fast Start! Set a winning tradition. It lasts a lifetime.

How to Start-Up the System

1. **Surround Your New Leaders with People from Their Prospect List**
   - Identify and Qualify their Top 25-100 Prospect.
   - Help them mentally picture having these people on their team.

2. **Approach for BOP by Using "The Play"**
   - Learn to understand human nature.
   - Become a master inviter.
   - It's always "no" unless you ask.

3. **"Hold-a-Meeting" – Office, Prospect's Home, Your Home, etc**
   - Show total HGI story and opportunity.
   - Leave prospect with "something of value" to study and listen to.
   - Set definite time for follow-up interview.

4. **Follow-up Within 24 to 48 Hours (Speed Filters 1-4)**
   - Get them to come to you, if possible, and conduct the Get Started Interview from the LFS Manual.

5. **Fast Start the New Recruit (Speed Filters 5-8)**
   - Start them back at the beginning – surround them with new people – Step 1, etc.

6. **Duplication**
   - This takes you from building your business by addition only to building by multiplication.

Income is earned from the sale of HGI-authorized products and services. No income is earned for recruiting.

3 Traits of Successful Leaders

1. Focus   2. Motivation   3. Execution

The most important Leadership skill for all new HGI associates is mastering the invitation and becoming a mobile inviter. Review Step No. 2 to learn the Video Drop System and avoid the Scenario of Disaster. Work with your upline Leader to "Drill for Skill" to master controlling the point of contact. Your ability to contact and bring quality people to the BOP will determine your level of success in HGI.

3 Keys to Success

1. Become a student of the Leadership Format System
2. Make money at whatever level you are at.
3. Fight for your next promotion.

5 Steps to Turn Yourself into the Perfect Copy Machine

- Find a plan that works.
- Do it over and over again.
- The rapid repetition of simple things leads to an inevitable explosion.
- Develop a cookie-cutter exactness.
- Create a machine.

Standardized - Predictable - Profitable

For training and educational purposes only. Not to be used with the public.

67

HGI Promotion Guidelines

One of HGI's great uniqueness is the ability to control your own destiny. Unlike most companies, where the date of your next promotion is uncertain and in the hands of others, at HGI you have control over when and how high you can go.

First Step: Become an Associate (A)

- Complete 3 FNA/Dime+ FT sales/7,500 BV/RV pts. ABV applies.

- Recruit a total of 3 direct quality associates.

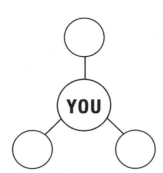

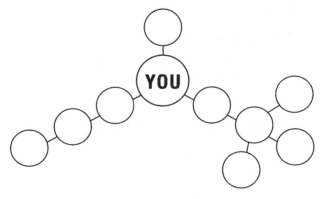

Second Step: Become a Field Associate (FA)

- Recruit a total of 6 quality team associates.

- Produce 25,000 BV/RV pts AV through your team in rolling 3 months / ABV Applies.

Third Step: Become a Senior Associate (SA)

- Recruit a total of 9 quality team associates.

- Produce 50,000 BV/RV pts through your team in rolling 3 months / ABV Applies.*

* See HGI Infinity Compensation Plan on page 73 for BV, ABV, RV, definitions and rules.

Fourth Step: Become a Marketing Director (MD)

- Recruit a total of 12 quality team associates.

- Produce 100,000 BV/RV pts through your team in rolling 3 months / ABV Applies.*

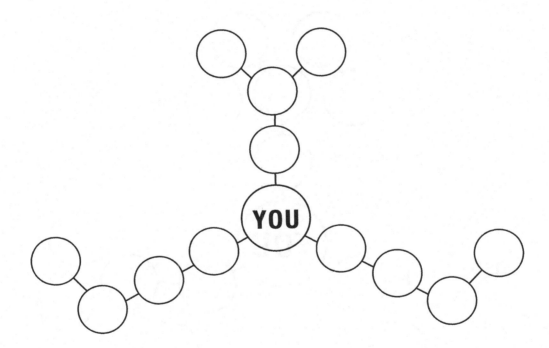

* See HGI Infinity Compensation Plan on page 73 for BV, ABV, RV, definitions and rules.

For training and educational purposes only. Not to be used with the public.

69

Fifth Step: Become a Regional Marketing Director (RMD)

- Recruit a total of 20 quality team associates.

- Produce 200,000 BV/RV pts through your team in rolling 3 months / ABV Applies.*

- Complete Builder's Exchange process.

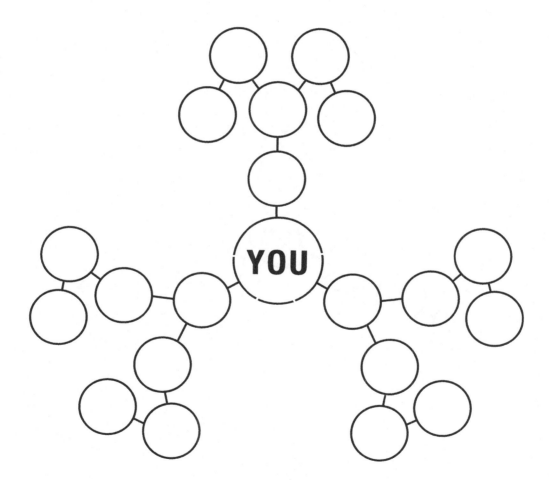

* See HGI Infinity Compensation Plan on page 73 for BV, ABV, RV, definitions and rules.

Sixth Step: Become a Senior Field Chairman (SFC)

- Build 2 Direct Qualified RMD Legs +

- Produce 300,000 ABV/RV pts thru 6th Gen. RMDs in any 90-day period.

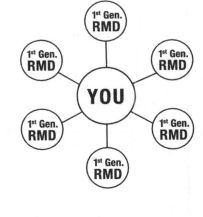

Seventh Step: Become an Executive Field Chairman (EFC)

- Build 4 Direct Qualified RMD Legs +

- Produce 600,000 ABV/RV pts thru 6th Gen. RMDs in any 90-day period.

Eighth Step: Become a Senior Executive Field Chairman (SEFC)

- Build 6 Direct Qualified RMD Legs +

- Produce 900,000 ABV/RV pts thru 6th Gen. RMDs in any 90-day period.

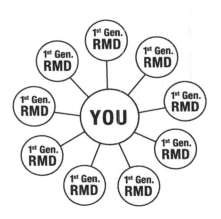

Ninth Step: Become a CEO Marketing Director (CEO MD)

- Build 10 Direct Qualified RMD Legs +

- 1.2 million ABV/RV pts thru 6th Gen. RMDs in any 90-day period.

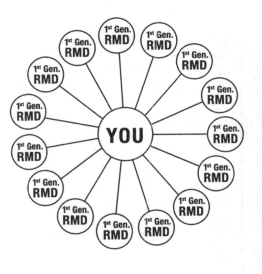

Promote-Me Worksheet

	New Recruit	Date Licensed	New Client	Points on Sale
1.				
2.				
3.				
4.				
5.				
6.				
7.				
8.				
9.				
10.				
11.				
12.				
13.				
14.				
15.				
16.				
17.				
18.				
19.				
20.				
21.				
22.				
23.				
24.				
25.				

 **Infinity Compensation Plan**

The Most Powerful Compensation Plan in the Industry

Promotion Level	Commission Levels	Promotion Standards
(TA) Training Associate	Scholarship Basic - $1,000 Adv - $2,000	Complete HGI Scholarship/Obtain License Minimum 3 Field Training Sales Minimum 3 Direct Recruits
(A) Associate	**40%**	3 Field Training Sales 3 Direct Recruits 7500 BV/RV in Rolling 3 months/ ABV Applies
(FA) Field Associate	**50%**	6 Team Recruits 25,000 BV/RV Rolling 3 months ABV Applies
(SA) Senior Associate	**60%**	9 Team Recruits 50,000 BV/RV Rolling 3 months ABV Applies
(MD) Marketing Director	**70%**	12 Team Recruits 100,000 BV/RV Rolling 3 months ABV Applies
(RMD) Regional Marketing Director	**80%**	20 Team Recruits 200,000 BV/RV Rolling 3 months ABV Applies

RMD Base Shop

Generational Overrides

Generations	Percent
1st Gen. RMD & Up	10.00%
2nd Gen. RMD & Up	5.00%
3rd Gen. RMD & Up	4.00%
4th Gen. RMD & Up	3.00%
5th Gen. RMD & Up	1.00%
6th Gen. RMD & Up	.75%
Total	**23.75%**

Quality Business Bonus

Up to 3.25% Based on quality production, quality recruits and maintaining high persistency.

Senior Executive Infinity Overrides

Level		Infinity Bonus	
(SFC) Senior Field Chairman	**81%**	1%	2 Direct Qualified RMD Legs + 300,000 (ABV/RV) thru 6th Gen. RMDs in any 90-day period.
(EFC) Executive Field Chairman	**82%**	2%	4 Direct Qualified RMD Legs + 600,000 (ABV/RV) thru 6th Gen. RMDs in any 90-day period.
(SEFC) Sr. Executive Field Chairman	**84%**	4%	6 Direct Qualified RMD Legs + 900,000 (ABV/RV) thru 6th Gen. RMDs in any 90-day period.
(CEO MD) CEO Marketing Director	**85%**	5%	10 Direct Qualified RMD Legs + 1.2 m (ABV/RV) thru 6th Gen. RMDs in any 90-day period.

BV = Business Value
1 point for every dollar commissionable premium.

ABV = Adjusted Business Business Value
No more than 1/3 of promotion requirements can come from any one leg.

RV = Recruiting Value
3 levels - combined with BV on all Leader Board reports, contests, promotions, etc.
Bronze Package Associate: earn 250 RV points for each new recruit.
Silver Package Associate: earn 500 RV points for each new recruit.
Gold Package Associate: earn 1,000 RV points for each new recruit.

RMD Equivalency
After you have fully qualified for an RMD promotion, every 150,000 issued and paid RMD Base Shop ABV/RV in any 90-day period will serve as the equivalent of one RMD leg promotion requirement for all Senior Executive promotions.

© 2015 Hegemon Group International™

Infinity Compensation Plan Description

HGI has one of the most powerful compensation and promotion plans in marketing today. We offer a unique blend of Fast Start Bonuses, Personal Contracts, Base Shop Overrides, Generational Overrides, Infinity Overrides and an Equity Sharing Credit Program that give you many exciting ways to make money with HGI.

Personal Production Contracts —40-85%

HGI offers great personal production contracts from 40-85%.

Base Shop Overrides —Up to 45%

When you obtain the RMD (80%) level, up to CEO MD (85%) level, this will allow you to have a Base Shop override spread of up to 45% on all new Associates and above in your Base Shop. (Base Shop Overrides available for Silver and Gold Package Associates only).

Generational Overrides —Total of 23.75%

Generational Overrides are earned once you become an RMD or higher and are based on what "generation" a leader is to you — with a total payout of 23.75%. For example, an RMD who personally reports to you would be 1st Generation and an RMD who reports to him/her would be 2nd Generation to you and so on. Generational Overrides are in addition to Infinity Overrides and are paid out monthly. (Generational Overrides available for Silver and Gold Package Associates only).

Generational Levels	Override
1st Generation RMD Base Shop	10.00%
2nd Generation RMD Base Shop	5.00%
3rd Generation RMD Base Shop	4.00%
4th Generation RMD Base Shop	3.00%
5th Generation RMD Base Shop	1.00%
6th Generation RMD Base Shop	0.75%
TOTAL	23.75%

REQUIREMENTS

In order to receive the full Generational Override each month, you must achieve 20,000 RMD Base Shop BV/RV points that month. RMDs or higher not achieving 20,000 RMD Base Shop BV/RV points in a particular month will receive 50% of their generational overrides for that particular month.

Infinity Overrides — 1%-5%

Infinity Overrides are paid to you through an unlimited number of levels. Commissions are calculated by simply subtracting the commission level of the person closest to you in your downline whose Promotion Level is lower than yours and is receiving credit from the generation of the sale — this will give you your Infinity Override percentage. (Infinity Overrides available for Silver and Gold Package Associates only).

Quality Business Bonus

Up to 3.25% Based on quality production, quality recruits and maintaining high persistency.

HGI Equity Sharing Credit Program

HGI Associates can earn Equity Share Credits that will allow them to participate in an Equity Share Pool in the event the company ever has a defining valuation event. A defining valuation event would include an IPO, Merger, or Sale of the Company, etc.

The HGI Equity Share Credit Program is not a security, it is not ownership in the company, and there is no guarantee there will be a defining valuation event.

For training and educational purposes only. Not to be used with the public.

74

Validation

RMDs must validate every 6 months on Leg and RMD Base Shop BV/RV requirements.

SFCs thru CEO MDs must validate every 12 months on Leg and RMD Base thru 6th Gen. BV/RV requirements. If an RMD does not meet validation requirements he/she would be placed one level lower on the HGI promotion platform until such time the validation requirements are met and the RMD would be re-established. (Re-validation must be achieved within 12 months).

Builder's Exchange

In order to be promoted to an RMD and benefit from a higher personal production contract, larger Infinity Override spreads and the ability to earn Generational Overrides, the newly promoted RMD must make a one-time "exchange" of a direct leg to his Promoting RMD (or higher) in order to receive the RMD promotion – this is called the Builder's Exchange Requirement. The Builder's Exchange leg is chosen by the promoting RMD. The one-time exchange now qualifies the newly promoted RMD to receive exchange legs from every new direct associate he or she promotes to RMD (see complete Builder's Exchange details starting on page 141).

ALL COMPENSATION LEVELS, RULES AND GUIDELINES ARE SUBJECT TO CHANGE WITHOUT NOTICE.

For training and educational purposes only. Not to be used with the public.

75

HGI
HEGEMON GROUP INTERNATIONAL

HGI Override Compensation Example

EXAMPLE BASED ON $5000 COMMISSIONABLE TARGET PREMIUM

HGI OVERRIDE COMPENSATION EXAMPLE

Promotion Level		Commission Level	Personal Sale Commission	HGI BASE SHOP OVERRIDE					HGI BASE SHOP + INFINITY OVERRIDE			
				Associate 40%	Field Associate 50%	Senior Associate 60%	Marketing Director 70%	Regional Marketing Diretor 80%	Senior Field Chairman 81%	Executive Field Chairman 82%	Senior Executive Field Chairman 84%	CEO Marketing Director 85%
Associate	A	40%	$2,000		$500	$1,000	$1,500	$2,000	$2,050	$2,100	$2,200	$2,250
Field Associate	FA	50%	$2,500			$500	$1,000	$1,500	$1,550	$1,600	$1,700	$1,750
Senior Associate	SA	60%	$3,000				$500	$1,000	$1,050	$1,100	$1,200	$1,250
Marketing Director	MD	70%	$3,500					$500	$550	$600	$700	$750
Regional Marketing Director	RMD	80%	$4,000						$50	$100	$200	$250
Senior Field Chairman	SFC	81%	$4,050							$50	$150	$200
Executive Field Chairman	EFC	82%	$4,100								$100	$150
Senior Executive Field Chairman	SEFC	84%	$4,200									$50
CEO Marketing Director	CEO MD	85%	$4,250									

HGI GENERATIONAL OVERRIDES

Generations	Override	
1st Gen RMD & UP	10%	$500
2nd Gen RMD & UP	5%	$250
3rd Gen RMD & UP	4%	$200
4th Gen RMD & UP	3%	$150
5th Gen RMD & UP	1%	$50
6th Gen RMD & UP	0.75%	$37.50

Refer to: Income Projections in HGI Back Office

Master the Art of Field Building

Three HGI Absolutes

In order to participate in company contests, incentive trips, bonus pools, equity sharing credit pool or any company recognition programs and elite clubs, you must implement:

1. Every new associate must immediately sign up with HGI.
2. Every new associate must immediately be assigned a Field Builder and complete all field training requirements.
3. Every new associate must immediately have at least one new recruit.

The No. 1 responsibility of every leader in HGI – from Associate to CEO MD – is to be a Field Builder.

- The Field Builder is responsible for training the new recruit:
    - Prospecting and Video Drop System –" The Play"
    - A Winning Presentation
    - Get Started Interview
    - Making the Sale

- Field Build the new associate with the goal of having 5-10 new recruits in the first few weeks.
- Input a minimum of 3 qualified field training sales.

Manage activity for you and your Field Builders.

- Set, maintain and follow-up on standards of excellence.
    - Field Build three to four nights per week and Saturdays - 10 presentations a week.

Field Builder Standards of Excellence
Associate Results when teamed with a Field Builder

	Video Drops/Week	Presentations/ Week	Recruits/ Week	FNAs/ Week	Closed Trans/Week	Income (50%)/Week
Poor	0-9	0-4	0	0	0	$0
Fair	10-14	5-7	1-2	1-2	1	$1,000
Good	15-20	8-10	3-4	3-4	2	$2,000
Great	21-29	11-19	4-5	4-5	3-4	$4,000
Excellent	30+	20+	6+	6+	5+	$5,000+

Personal Standards of Excellence: 10 Video Drops
5 Presentations
2 Recruits and
2 Transactions per week.

Field Building

Every RMD must have at least one Certified Field Builder. HGI Success Ratio: 1 CFB for every 15 recruits.

The Four Key Responsibilities of Field Building
1. Prospecting and Video Drop System ("The Play")
2. A Winning Presentation (Leaders With Vision flipchart)
3. Get Started Interview
4. Making the Sale

How the RMD Builds Field Builders
1. They learn by observing first-hand what you do.
2. Drill For Skill - role play each step with them.
3. Make sure they master each step. (Inspect and certify their ability to complete each step.)
4. RMD delegates responsibility one step at a time.
5. Monitor results to know their effectiveness.

Accountability of Field Builders
Field Builders must update and submit weekly to RMD:
1. Eight Speed Filter Check List
2. Field Builder Match-Up Report
3. Video Movement/Circulation Report for upcoming week for each trainee on Field Builder Match-Up Report
4. Team Leadership Check List

The Definition of a HGI Field Builder:
1. Field Recruiting - the continuous opening of outlets.
2. Field Training - the movement of volume production through the outlets.

Certified Field Builder Requirements:
1. You must be a Quality Associate:
    – Signed up with HGI and all product providers that you want to represent.
    – Complete field training requirements.
    – Have at least one recruit who has signed up with all companies.
2. You must master these skills and be certified by your RMD:
    – Prospecting and the Video Drop System - " The Play"
    – A Winning Presentation - Leaders With Vision flipchart.
    – The Get Started Interview.
    – Making the Sale.
3. You must be in total alignment with HGI and use all of our communication tools:
    – Associate login section of HGICrusade.com and Company Email
    – The Leader Network
    – HGI Text Network
    – LFSMAX Online Marketing System, HGIUniversity.com and HGISuccessStore.com
The RMD must take full responsibility that each Certified Field Builder has met all requirements.

Field Builder Training and Accountability

Each RMD must meet with their Field Builders on a weekly basis to monitor the progress of all new recruits in the RMD Base. The following is the suggested outline to be used for the meeting agenda.

1. Review Eight Speed Filter Reports

– Review the Speed Filter progress of each new recruit.
– Discuss and schedule follow-up to make sure each new recruit completes their next step.
  (New prospects should remain on the Eight Speed Filter Report no more than seven days.)

2. Review Field Building Match-Up Reports

– Make sure every new recruit is on the report.
– Check last week's activity for each recruit.
– Check last week's Field Building personal activity.
– Check number of videos to be dropped this week.

3. Review Video Circulation Report

– Each recruit on Field Building Match-Up Report should have at least ten names on this report.
– Review and discuss last week's numbers.

4. Review Leadership Check List.

– Discuss and assign follow-up to make sure new recruit meets all requirements on the Check List.

5. Assign responsibilities for the next BOP, using the BOP Leadership Assignments Form.

6. Drill for Skill.

– Week No. 1 – Prospecting/Video Drop - " The Play"
– Week No. 2 – The Presentation/The BOP
– Week No. 3 – The Start-Up/Getting Started Interview
– Week No. 4 – Making the Sale/Mastering the Art of Field Building
– Week No. 5 – Forward - Start the Cycle Again

Section II — BUILDERS MINDSET

HGI™
HEGEMON GROUP INTERNATIONAL

The Eight Speed Filter Check List

	Name	Phone Number	Inviter's Name	FILTER 1 Stay After BOP/Mozone	FILTER 2 Get the Kit	FILTER 3 Commit to Get Started Interview	FILTER 4 Complete Interview/Sign Up	FILTER 5 Develop Prospect List	FILTER 6 Set Goals/ Business Plan	FILTER 7 FNA/ Internal Consumption	FILTER 8 Match-Up Field Building
1											
2											
3											
4											
5											
6											
7											
8											
9											
10											
11											
12											
13											
14											
15											
16											
17											
18											
19											
20											
21											
22											
23											
24											

(New prospects should remain on the Eight Speed Filter Check List no more than seven days.)

The Magic of the Match-Up System

The Match-Up System is the key to your ability to continue to get wide with new direct leaders. The tendency of some leaders is to not hire too many new associates because they feel they won't have the time necessary to get in the field and effectively work with them. The Match-Up System solves this dilemma by allowing you to "match-up" your new associates with other licensed leaders to help get the job done.

Match-Up Power Principles

- Allows every new associate to get in the field within 24 to 48 hours with an experienced leader
- Helps retain your existing team by allowing them to make money field training new associates
- Increases activity for the whole organization
- Generates points for promotions
- Provides needed experience for all associates — "old" and "new"
- Helps to avoid a small-thinking mentality
- 50% of something is better than 100% of nothing
- Builds leaders

There are three ways to Match-Up:

1. Internal - within your base shop
2. Internal Hierarchy - with other leaders on your team
3. Inter-Hierarchy - with other leaders in HGI

Match-up experienced leaders with new, unlicensed associates.

The two most important titles in HGI are:

- **Field Trainer**
- **Dynasty Builder**

Match-Up Rules and Guidelines

1. Everybody must have uniform presentations - duplicable, easy, approved with a total focus on suitability.
2. Must agree to automatically recruit after the sale at all times.
3. Must have a trainer's code. Don't show or communicate any disrespect for other trainers.
4. Split 50/50 - All Match-Up sales are split 50/50 between the recruiter and the field trainer. The trainee also receives education, training & professional development.
5. Trainer must communicate with trainee prior to appointment - reconfirm appointment and pre-qualify client.
6. Both recruiter/leader and field trainer must coach trainee on dos and don'ts during presentation. A trainee cannot participate in the discussion or presentation of the products offered by HGI.
7. Do not cancel an appointment with trainee or client under any circumstances - trainer must fulfill obligation or make arrangements for another trainer.
8. Always send field trainer to solid appointments.
9. If you use inter-hierarchy, inform them of rules and guidelines and get an agreement first.
10. Reputation is everything - do not abuse the system.

Section II — BUILDERS MINDSET

The Match-Up Multiples

Personally recruit **10** wide as quickly as possible. Then, get each recruit matched up at least three nights per week.

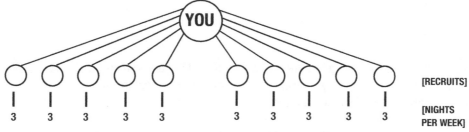

[RECRUITS]

[NIGHTS PER WEEK]

Ten recruits matched up three nights per week gives you **30** field-training nights per week.

Then, if **each** new recruit recruits three and the original **10** and the new **30** work three nights per week, that is **120** nights of recruiting presentations being made per week.

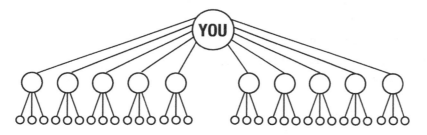

For training and educational purposes only. Not to be used with the public.

82

FIELD BUILDER MATCH-UP REPORT

HGI — HEGEMON GROUP INTERNATIONAL

Field Builder _____

RMD _____

Week Of: _____

Trainee Name	NEXT WEEK'S VIDEO DROPS	VIDEO DROPS		CONTACTS		PRESENTATIONS		RECRUITS		FNAs		REFERRALS		OTHER	
		WEEK	MTD	WEEK	MTD	WEEK	MTD	WEEK	MTD	WEEK	MTD	WEEK	MTD	WEEK	MTD
Field Builder Personal Activity ------>															
1															
2															
3															
4															
5															
6															
7															
8															
9															
10															
11															
12															
13															
14															
TOTALS															

Field Builder updates and turns into RMD weekly.

1. Eight Speed Filter Check List
2. Field Builder Match-Up Report
3. Video Circulation Report for each new recruit
4. Team Leadership Check List

The Field Builder is responsible for driving activity.

Team Leadership Check List

RMD _____

Promotions/Awards	Promoted to RMD
	Promoted to SA
	Promoted to FA
	Fast Start Award
Marketing Tools/Events	Product Provider Links
	HGI University Active
	LFSMAX Gold Active
	Register for Next Event
Own Products	Non-Licensed Provider
	Insurance/Annuity
Field Building Certified	Making the Sale
	Get Started Interview
	A Winning Presentation
	Prospecting/Video Drop System
Match-Up	Match-Up Sales
	Field Builder
Non-Licensed Providers	IC/Customer Sales
	Product Provider Training
HFG	Getting Licensed?
	IC Sale
	FNA
	Contracted/Appointed
	My License Profile
HGI	3 Field Training Sales
	Demonstrated ability to login to all HGI websites
	At least 100 leads loaded into LFSMAX Gold System
	At least 100 leads on list
	W-9 Submitted
	Ordered HGI Business Cards
	Ordered Brochures for "The Play and Decision Kits"
	Complete 8 Speed Filters
	Recruit Name

Field Builder updates and turns into RMD weekly

1. Eight Speed Filter Check List
2. Field Builder Match-Up Report
3. Video Circulation Report for each new recruit
4. Team Leadership Check List

How to Build a Big Base Shop

The future of HGI belongs to those who build big Base Shops.

Why build a big base shop?

- A big Base Shop is the originating source of power, prestige, income and the key to the big time.
- A leadership factory: Build leaders and teams will come. This is the original source of your hierarchy.
- Compensation: The majority is in the Base Shop. Let the compensation program of the company tell you where you need to be spending your time.
- Base Shop ———▶ Super Base ———▶ Hierarchy ———▶ Dynasty

The Magnificent 7 Commitments to Building a Big Base Shop

1. **Personal Commitment**
   - Decide you are going to build a big Base Shop and communicate that to your team.
   - Tell your team that you'll be #1, and they'll be #1

2. **Personal Recruiting Commitment**
   - The wider the better
   - The faster the better
   - Collapse time frames
   - Profitable

3. **Personal Leadership Commitment**
   - You be the leader
   - Build leaders
   - Accelerate the building of leaders
   - Think big, but keep it simple

4. **System Commitment**
   - Rapid duplication
   - Build a machine

5. **Match-Up Commitment**
   - Master the Magic of the Match-Up System. (see page 81)

6. **Commitment to be Positive and Optimistic**
   - Example: Magnet - attracts or repels.
   - People like to be around positive and motivated people.

7. **Commitment to Endure**
   - You must keep on repeating the LFS again and again, even when you are bored with it.

Basic Building Block: 4x4 (4 Wide and 4 Deep)

For every four, you'll find one leader.

Spend the majority of your time at the most critical part.

Communication - Go Deep

7 Steps

1. Recognize and praise, then motivate.
   Tell other teammates' success stories.
2. Ask 20 percent.
3. Personal: family, job, etc...
4. Business: HGI recruits and CEO MD Club
5. Listen 80 percent.
6. Give instructions and guidance, then challenge.
7. Learn to sell Big Dreams for their future.

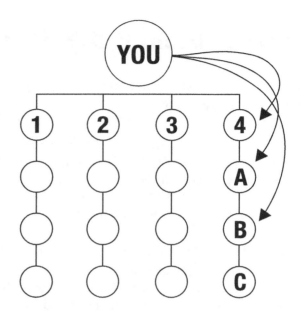

Base Shop Strategies

Always maintain a big Base Shop:

- Demonstrate and build multiple Base Shops throughout major locations around the country.
- Produce at least one strong, direct new RMD each month from this Base Shop.

Weekly Activity Plan

" Manage activity, but focus on results."

"Monitor = Money"

LEADERS	PERFORMANCE PROJECTIONS						SUNDAY ACTUAL RESULTS REVIEW TOTALS
	MON	TUES	WED	THURS	FRI	SAT	
1							
2							
3							
4							
5							
6							
7							
8							
9							
10							
11							
12							
13							
14							
15							

RMDs AND UP CALL EACH OF THEIR KEY LEADERS EVERY SUNDAY NIGHT TO:

1. Motivate and **PULL** them **UP**.
2. Get their **COMMITMENT** to work this week toward the goals they set when they joined HGI.
3. Complete this **PROJECTION CHART** for the upcoming week:
     a) Time blocks committed to work.
     b) Type of activity - personal work, field training new associates or designated extra field training assigned by RMD.
     c) Names of trainees and whether it's a one-on-one BOP; group BOP or Product Presentation.
4. Excitedly share with them the HGI "Good News."
5. Review prospect lists and key personnel with them.
6. Keep them on a recruiting track, attending the BOP.
7. Review their actual field activity from previous week on the chart.

Making the Sale

Winning Principles

- Remember, every presentation is a recruiting presentation first.
- Feel good about yourself, have a positive attitude and dress for success.
- Feel good about the company. You must be totally committed to our concepts.
- Sell our concepts by using our "Leaders with Vision" presentation.
- People need our help. Be a crusader. Be enthusiastic and excited about the good that we do.
- Always get referrals - someone who has bought from you will buy from you again, and is willing to refer you to other people as well.
- There are only two reasons why a client in the right market will not do business with you:
    - They don't believe you.
    - They don't understand you.
- Understand up front that 20 to 30% of people reserve the right to make the wrong decision no matter what you do and you should not take it personally.
- You must see both the husband and the spouse or significant other. They both need and deserve to know about the opportunity.
- You must be properly certified/licensed with the product provider companies to market products.
- Be sure you use only current, approved sales material.
- Everyone is a recruit until proven differently.

Keys to Making An Appointment

- The best sources of warm market appointments:
    - Prospects after a BOP (personal and team)
    - Appointments set directly from a prospect list
    - Referrals from satisfied clients
- The appointment can be handled at the home, the office or a restaurant.
- You control when the appointment is to be set. Use the " -ish" principle, (" I'll be there 6-ish, 7-ish, 8:30-ish," etc.). Build in time to be a little early or a little late.

Preparation

- Have all your materials with you:
    - Current, company-approved HGI BOP flipchart presentation, and additional support materials
- Make sure your trainee (if training) knows his or her support role.
- Know your potential client as well as possible.

For training and educational purposes only. Not to be used with the public.

88

Making A Winning Presentation

- Upon arrival, show friendly, low-key interest in the client.
- Make the presentation at the kitchen table, if in the home.
- Again, whether the presentation is made at the home or office, both spouses need to be there.
- During your presentation, always make eye contact.
- If you are there on a client referral, use the client's name and ask how they know them.
- Make the "Leaders with Vision" presentation.
- During the presentation, involve the client on every page by asking questions and encouraging and listening to comments.
- Use tie down statements like, " That makes sense, doesn't it? You'd like to save this kind of money, wouldn't you?" and to reinforce your referral position ("Aren't you glad _____ recommended that we get together tonight?," or "_____ liked that part, too."), etc.
- Get a strong commitment. (" If we're as good as we say we are, is there any reason we couldn't do business?")
- Select products best suited to fit their needs.
- Make Sale, get App filled out, arrange for Medical tests as required.
- Get referrals.
- Invite the new client to your next BOP.
- Leave HGI *Products and Services* brochure and *How to Win the Money Game* brochure.
- Thank them for their business and let them know you are available to serve their future needs.
- The first presentation should last 30 minutes.

Follow-Up

- Drop thank you note or card in the mail to show your appreciation.
- Follow-up with client to make sure App is submitted. Stay in touch with insurance company to deliver policy and get client sign-off as appropriate.

Ongoing Client Services

- Stay in touch - most people will consider some of our other products and services at a later date.

For training and educational purposes only. Not to be used with the public.

89

Achieve Your Career Best Effort (C.B.E.)

All successful Leaders constantly strive to set a new standard for their own "Career Best Effort". The "new" must always beat the "old" you. All Leaders must have a clear picture of where their business has been, where it is now, and most importantly, what aspect of their business should receive their fullest concentration in the future.

Career Best Effort Actions are broken down into two areas:

1. Manage Activity   2. Focus On Results

Manage Activity, But Focus on Results

Activity	Results

1. Prospecting
2. Contacting
   -Brochure/Video Link (HGIPlay.com)
   -Inviting to BOPs
   -Setting up appointments
3. BOPs
   - Group BOPs
   - One-on-Ones
4. Make Winning Sales Presentations/Field Building
5. Collecting Financial Data
6. HGI Recruits
7. FNA's / DIME+
8. Advance Points on Leader's Reports
	1. Product Company Sign-ups
	2. Product Company Certified/Licensed
	3. Closed Business
	4. Cash Flow
	5. Closed Points on Leader's Reports
	6. Win Trips/Contests
	7. Register and attend Convention and Top Gun
	8. RMD-CEOMD Promotions
	9. Success Society Watches
	10. Champion's Club Rings
	11. Diamond Club Members
	12. Hall of Fame Members
	13. Hall of Legends Members
	14. Chairman's Circle of Honor Members

Key Areas of Focus to Achieve Your Goals

Define Reality & Develop Goals

- Where has your business been?   • Where is it now?

Monitoring & Accountability

- Instill discipline and accountability as a foundation for success.
- Teach your Leaders to monitor performance on a consistent and proactive basis.
- Teach your Leaders to understand that "Building Block" actions lead to "Direct Productivity" actions.

Career Best Effort

- Consistent, sustainable growth eventually leads to quantum growth.
- C.B.E. requires constant awareness of past and current performance.
- Establish key areas of measurement.
- Compete against yourself - the best you're capable of.
- Constant focus on C.B.E. assures complacency won't creep into an organization's efforts.

Develop a winning business plan to develop a winning business.

HGI Speed Calendar

Collapse Time Frames/Compress Activity

"For a thousand years in thy sight are but as yesterday."

- Psalms 90:4

What a powerful paradigm - a thousand years on earth is but a day in the sight of the Lord.

While we'll never be able to collapse time like this, we can become Possibility Thinkers and Impossibility Achievers by compressing a decade into one year ... one year into three months ... three months into one week one week into one day ... and one day into three mini-days.

	MONDAY	TUESDAY	WEDNES-	THURSDAY	FRIDAY	SATUR-
7 a.m. TO noon	MINI-DAY **1** Minimum 5 Direct Contacts	MINI-DAY **4** Minimum 5 Direct Contacts	MINI-DAY **7** Minimum 5 Direct Contacts	MINI-DAY **1** Minimum 5 Direct Contacts	MINI-DAY **1** Minimum 5 Direct Contacts	MINI-DAY **1** Minimum 5 Direct Contacts
12:01 to 6 p.m.	MINI-DAY **2** Minimum 5 Direct Contacts	MINI-DAY **5** Minimum 5 Direct Contacts	MINI-DAY **8** Minimum 5 Direct Contacts	MINI-DAY **1** Minimum 5 Direct Contacts	MINI-DAY **1** Minimum 5 Direct Contacts	MINI-DAY **1** Minimum 5 Direct Contacts
6:01 p.m. to midnight	MINI-DAY **3** PRIME TIME 7 - 10 p.m. Minimum 5 Direct Contacts	MINI-DAY **6** PRIME TIME 7 - 10 p.m. Minimum 5 Direct Contacts	MINI-DAY **9** PRIME TIME 7 - 10 p.m. Minimum 5 Direct Contacts	MINI-DAY **1** PRIME TIME 7 - 10 p.m. Minimum 5 Direct Contacts	MINI-DAY **1** PRIME TIME 7 - 10 p.m. Minimum 5 Direct Contacts	MINI-DAY **1** PRIME TIME 7 - 10 p.m. Minimum 5 Direct Contacts

Total Combustion Super Blitz Campaign

"I expect every HGI RMD/Leader to MAX-OUT all 6 days (18 Mini-Days) each week for one full 90-Day Madman Cycle." - Hubert Humphrey

If you are not yet full-time with HGI, simply fill in the time slots which you have to devote to building your HGI business.

HGI Speed Calendar

_____
(Month)

Monday	Tuesday	Wednesday	Thursday	Friday	Saturday
Mini-Day **1** 7:00 ___ 8:00 ___ 9:00 ___ 10:00 ___ 11:00 ___	Mini-Day **4** 7:00 ___ 8:00 ___ 9:00 ___ 10:00 ___ 11:00 ___	Mini-Day **7** 7:00 ___ 8:00 ___ 9:00 ___ 10:00 ___ 11:00 ___	Mini-Day **10** 7:00 ___ 8:00 ___ 9:00 ___ 10:00 ___ 11:00 ___	Mini-Day **13** 7:00 ___ 8:00 ___ 9:00 ___ 10:00 ___ 11:00 ___	Mini-Day **16** 7:00 ___ 8:00 ___ 9:00 ___ 10:00 ___ 11:00 ___
Mini-Day **2** 12:00 ___ 1:00 ___ 2:00 ___ 3:00 ___ 4:00 ___ 5:00 ___	Mini-Day **5** 12:00 ___ 1:00 ___ 2:00 ___ 3:00 ___ 4:00 ___ 5:00 ___	Mini-Day **8** 12:00 ___ 1:00 ___ 2:00 ___ 3:00 ___ 4:00 ___ 5:00 ___	Mini-Day **11** 12:00 ___ 1:00 ___ 2:00 ___ 3:00 ___ 4:00 ___ 5:00 ___	Mini-Day **14** 12:00 ___ 1:00 ___ 2:00 ___ 3:00 ___ 4:00 ___ 5:00 ___	Mini-Day **17** 12:00 ___ 1:00 ___ 2:00 ___ 3:00 ___ 4:00 ___ 5:00 ___
Mini-Day **3** — Prime Time 7:00 p.m.-10:00 p.m. 6:00 ___ 7:00 ___ 8:00 ___ 9:00 ___ 10:00 ___ 11:00 ___ 12:00 ___	Mini-Day **6** — Prime Time 7:00 p.m.-10:00 p.m. 6:00 ___ 7:00 ___ 8:00 ___ 9:00 ___ 10:00 ___ 11:00 ___ 12:00 ___	Mini-Day **9** — Prime Time 7:00 p.m.-10:00 p.m. 6:00 ___ 7:00 ___ 8:00 ___ 9:00 ___ 10:00 ___ 11:00 ___ 12:00 ___	Mini-Day **12** — Prime Time 7:00 p.m.-10:00 p.m. 6:00 ___ 7:00 ___ 8:00 ___ 9:00 ___ 10:00 ___ 11:00 ___ 12:00 ___	Mini-Day **15** — Prime Time 7:00 p.m.-10:00 p.m. 6:00 ___ 7:00 ___ 8:00 ___ 9:00 ___ 10:00 ___ 11:00 ___ 12:00 ___	Mini-Day **18** — Prime Time 7:00 p.m.-10:00 p.m. 6:00 ___ 7:00 ___ 8:00 ___ 9:00 ___ 10:00 ___ 11:00 ___ 12:00 ___

7:00 a.m. to 12:00 Noon
 Minimum 5 Direct
 Contacts per Mini Day

12:01 p.m. to 6:00 p.m.
 Minimum 5 Direct
 Contacts per Mini Day

6:01 p.m. to 12:00 Midnight
 Minimum 5 Direct
 Contacts per Mini Day

HEGEMON GROUP INTERNATIONAL

SECTION II BUILDERS MINDSET

Step 6 Duplication

The Rapid Repetition of the HGI Proven System

Purpose: To build a business using HGI's proven system whereby recruiting never stops.

To become a legend of the future, you must study the legends of the past.

The speed and exactness with which you copy the system will in large part determine your success in HGI. This cookie-cutter exactness must be duplicated throughout your team.

Remember two things:

> 1. *You will be paid to imitate, not create.*
> 2. *Marketing is the creation of the outlet and the movement of the product simultaneously.*

The key components of duplication include:

- ### The Magic of Compound Recruiting & Building

  Once you develop a Recruiter's Mentality and a Builders Mindset, you will be on your way to creating "A System Whereby Recruiting and Building Teams Never Stops."

  I. Recruiter's Mentality

  II. Builders Mindset

  III. Director of Motivation

- ### Turnkey Leadership Principles

  HGI's unparalleled Recognition and Reward Program is what separates HGI from every other business in the world today. It is critical to understand that recognition, communication and events are just as important to the HGI Leadership Format System as training. You must become a Director of Motivation.

- ### World-Class Support

  This section covers how to set up an office, the use of technology and other resources to build your business.

The Magic of Compound Recruiting & Building

A Recruiters Mentality

Recruiting is an all-the-time thing. It is a "state of mind." Look for quantity, get quality. Remember, every prospect is a recruit until proven differently.

The Hold-A-Meeting System - Capture the Magic of Crowds

- The One-on-One BOP
- A Dynamic BOP

Average number of people per week at BOP = Average number of Base Shop sales per month.
Use a BOP Projection Sheet. If you don't prepare to have a good meeting — you won't. Always monitor the numbers.

A Builders Mindset

You are in the people building business. You must see yourself as a Leader of thousands, running a system with two main objectives:

1. Build a large network of outlets.
2. Build a large base of diversified product-using clients.*

This is your ultimate goal.

Build to Max-out Profits
1. "Wide"
2. "Deep"
3. "Wide" and "Deep"

Width = Profitability
Depth = Security

Primary: GO WIDE
Secondary: GO DEEP

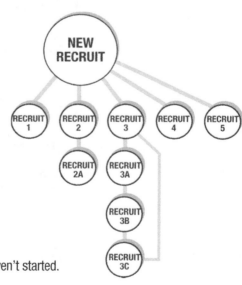

You can go Deep after you go Wide but you can't have depth in a leg you haven't started. You can control the planter, but you can't control the plant.

Building Keys

Don't resort to "panic management," which is caused by:
1. Lack of money.
2. Lack of activity.
3. Lack of a definite, second business philosophy.

Most people don't build a big marketing business because they suffer from No. 3.

> **"Always focus on going wide. Depth will follow. Remember, you can't have grandchildren until you have children."**
>
> — Hubert Humphrey

The Magic of Taprooting

The 3 Laws of Recruiting

1. A recruit isn't a recruit until he/she has a recruit.

Harness the Power of Geometric Progression

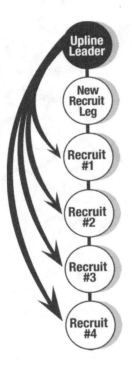

2. A recruit is not a leg until it is at least four deep.

3. A leg will become a team with a life of its own once you find at least 2 leaders.

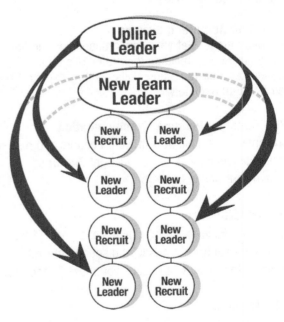

Building Outlets

1. Opening outlets is an all-the-time thing.
2. Have quantity to get quality.

Open Outlets and Move Products Simultaneously

Do not make the mistake of focusing on sales. You must think of opening outlets — "Aim at recruits...hit sales."

- Only 25% of the prospects on a target list will ever come to a BOP.
- If only 100 come to a BOP, you can be assured there are 500 to 600 more who should have come.
- Make sure to offer the opportunity to do an FNA/Internal Consumption Sale for these people.

The Super Taproot

The "Super Taproot" is a system for maximizing Taprooting, building permanent width by going temporarily deep to build Builders Exchanges (see pg.141-144). This system assures that you are always a do-it-first, wide at the top Leader with strong downline Leadership that assures geometric progression.

This is the key to building wide, deep and geometric.

Keys to Taprooting

Taproot Irrigation System

FRS - Field Recruiting System
Field Recruiting – Get your new prospects in the field to immediately begin building their team. It's important that they master their recruiting skills, so they can start building their team immediately.

CPC - Constant Personal Communication
Constantly communicate with your Leaders and new recruits. Everybody joining your team must get CPC from you and your upline Leaders.

FTF – Face-to-Face
See people "Face-to-Face." Uplines must be FTF with downlines. Set appointments and spend time with people all the time. As a Leader, you must Taproot down.

RTR – Reverse Taproot
Reverse Taproot – You must bring your downline to spend time with successful Leaders and attend big events. Have the mindset to reverse the process instead of waiting for Leaders to come to your downline. You must Taproot up.

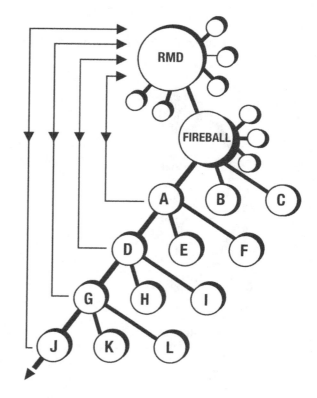

"Recruit & Motivate" — The System to Simplify and Multiply

Recruit

Run a system whereby recruiting never stops:

1. Personal speed width = You must commit to and execute four consecutive 90-Day Madman Cycles of personal recruiting/front-line expansion.

2. You've got to constantly have geometric recruiting through your ambitious Leaders and constantly identify, at all levels, your recruiting capacitors who can take a big-time recruiting charge from you.

3. The key to exploding big is to build and maintain a minimum 50,000 BV pts. RMD base each month. This is the ONLY WAY you can consistently produce new 1st Generation Senior Associates/RMDs.

Motivate

Run a system whereby motivation never stops:

1. Stretch their vision, then motivate them.

2. There's a big difference between a motivated person and a great motivator.

3. To be a great Director of Motivation, you have to constantly, strategically direct your people to the proper environment, atmosphere, places, Leaders and events that will stretch their vision for you.

4. You can't stretch your own vision, you must submit yourself to great Leaders and great visionaries to stretch it for you.

Depth Force

In order for the Super Taproot System to work, YOU have to become the "Depth Force" that pushes strength and vitality through each level of your organization.

Make sure every new person understands:

1. You're going to surround him/her with good people.

   Surround yourself with people — teach them how to recruit and train.

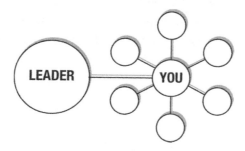

2. You're going to surround his/her people with good people.

   Surround your people with people — teach others "how to teach, how to recruit, and how to train."

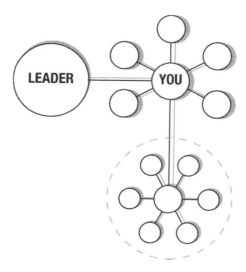

To build a Super Hierarchy, you must work Deep and Wide at the same time. You'll identify the more ambitious recruits and be able to "Taproot" through them.

How to Build One Strong Leg

The Power of One Leg Driven Deep

By always helping a new person get just "one" new person at every level, you always position yourself for at least four more sales. And you have the potential for a Fireball Leader to pop up.

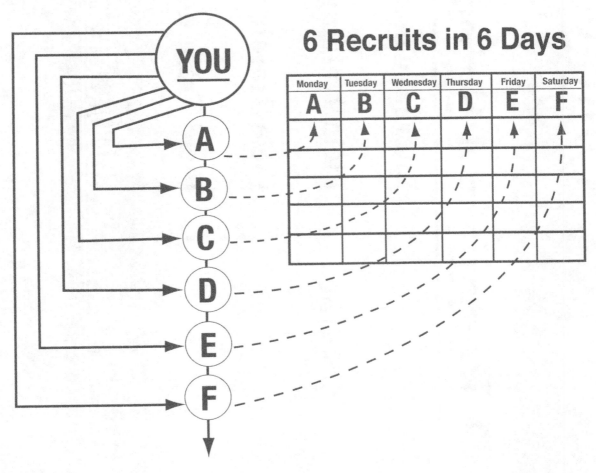

6 Recruits in 6 Days

Monday	Tuesday	Wednesday	Thursday	Friday	Saturday
A	B	C	D	E	F

Power Points

1. By always helping your new recruit at all levels get just "one" recruit, you position yourself for at least four more training sales and a potential new "Fireball" Leader.

2. By scheduling each new downline recruit a specific night on your field calendar, you can easily go four to five deep in seven to 14 days!

3. The probability is high that each recruit, whether strong or weak, can recruit at least one person.

The Power Of One Recruit

1 Recruit = 4 Sales

Recruit

4 Sales

- Internal Consumption
- Field Training/Match Up
- Field Training/Match Up
- Field Training/Match Up

1 Recruit = 4 Sales = $5,000 Compensation*

4 Sales = 10,000 BV Points

$5K compensation example based on RMD 80% Level, $10K Target Compensation & RMD split sales

Notes:

Two Main Focal Points to Win the Race for Outlets

1. Get more and more personal direct legs.
2. Get more and more people ("old" and "new") to BOPs.

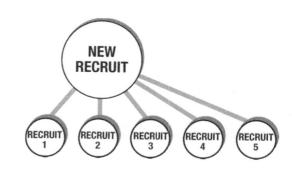

Success Formula:

Average Number of People Per Week at BOP = Average Number of Base Shop Sales Per Month

Manage Activity, But Focus on Results.

The only thing standing between you and your dreams coming true is the building of your distribution system.

Our Challenge to You ...

It all starts with you. You must first rally you, then rally your team. Double, triple and quadruple your personal width every 90 days! You set the pace for your team.

Five Wide to 50 Wide — All You Have to Change is You.

Which Leader Will You Be?

Build It Three Times

    1. Build it in your mind.

    2. Build it on paper.

    3. Build it!

The Tendency of Most Weaker Builders is to:

    1. Recruit them.

    2. Train them.

The Builders Mindset Says:

    1. Recruit them.

    2. Help them build teams, while training them how to recruit.

The Power of One

By getting just "one" recruit, you position yourself for at least 4 more training sales and a potential new "fireball" Leader. Remember, you are only one recruit away from an explosion.

Speed Width

Recruit in Bunches

When trying to build, how can you tell who will make it in this business? You can't. The people who are serious about winning and those who just give it lip service all look alike when you're first talking to them. That's why you should look for a BUNCH of people. There is just no way to accurately judge a person when you are trying to recruit him/her. No test has ever been devised that can measure the heart of a person.

The Magic of Hiring in Waves

You must develop a rhythm of recruiting at least three to 12 people personally every 30 to 45 days and invest as much time as possible with the ambitious people (the people with the most desire to win).

Go Wide Fast

Sixty Wide in Six Months

A person uses the sixty-wide-in-six-months worksheet on page 105 two ways. One is in the planning stage, in which he/she takes a pencil and fills in the names of people he/she thinks are going to be the next five or 10 people. Then, when he/she actually gets them, write their names in ink. Ask the person to turn it in every month. If it's got one name, fine. If it's the same name next month, fine. The point is to keep it in front of them, give them something to shoot for.

Whether you are shooting for 30 wide in six months, or 10 wide in six months, always project a plan. You can't help but get big FAST with that kind of a personal building effort.

Lots of People Doing a Little, Led by a Few Doing a Lot.

1. Give everyone an opportunity.
2. Give everyone examples of success.

The only way to overcome the negatives of the Law of Averages is to harness the power of the Law of High Numbers.

The Law of Averages at Work

Recruit 25 to 50 percent of all your prospects.

200 BOP attendees	=	50 new recruits
50 recruits	=	25 certified associates
25 associates	=	1 Regional Marketing Director
25 RMDs	=	1 Super Team Builder
7 to 10 Super Team Builders	=	Positioned for financial independence

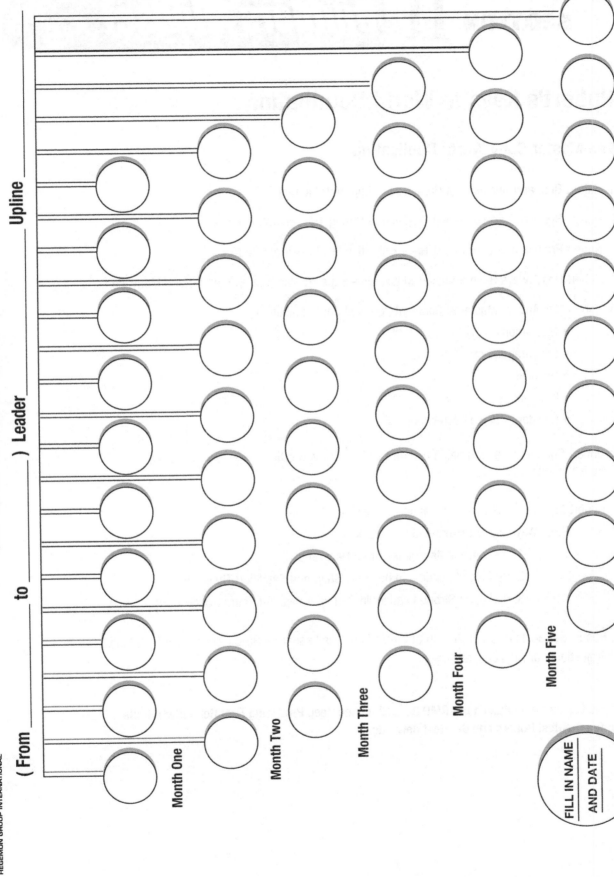

60 WIDE IN 6 MONTHS

(From _____ to _____) Leader _____ Upline

Month One

Month Two

Month Three

Month Four

Month Five

Month Six

FILL IN NAME
AND DATE

Section II — BUILDERS MINDSET

Hubert's Keys to World Domination

The Master Copy Worth Duplicating

1. Hubert Built and Sustained a Great Base Shop RMD Factory.

2. Hubert Built an Ever-Expanding Frontline of Strong 1st Generation RMDs.

3. Hubert Produced 8 to 10 Direct Giant Executive Field Chairman Teams.

4. Hubert Has Always Been a Master Motivator – Super Teams Run on High Octane Motivation.

5. Hubert Has Always Mastered Constant Personal Communication.
   - Motivation
   - Encouragement
   - Good News
   - Know-how
   - Constant Course Correction

6. Hubert Couldn't Live with being Average and Ordinary. He Didn't Just Want to be No. 1.
   He Needed to be No. 1.

7. Hubert Mastered a System for National Expansion.

   Three Ways Hubert Expanded his Business:

   1. He Transplanted Himself to a New Area
   2. He Raised Leaders in his Base Shop and Satellited Them Out.
   3. He Found Strong Leaders in Certain Areas and Built through Them.

8. Hubert Set Goals of Great Growth of Himself and His Leaders – He Constantly Set Possibility
   Projections for His Leaders.

**To the Leaders Who Build a Big RMD Base Shop and Keep Producing First Generation RMDs
Go the Greatest Honors and Greatest Rewards.**

Develop A "Builders Mindset"

"Master Builder" Building Contractor

1. Envisions the **completed** project **before** he/she starts to build.

2. Has blueprints **drawn** up in great **detail.**

3. Determines how much raw material/supplies/workers are needed to complete the project.

4. Determines how much it will cost to do the job.

5. Sets a **deadline** for completion.

6. Develops a written **business** plan to:

   a. Hire:
      Painters
      Brick Masons
      Plumbers
      Electricians
      Roofers
      Laborers
      Carpenters
      Subcontractors

   b. Negotiates a **constant and sufficient** cash flow to **finish** the job and stay in business (normally with a bank).

"Team Builder" HGI Field Leader

1. Has a **clear mental picture** of being the "Leader of Thousands."

2. Prepares a business plan to reach his/her goals.

3. Determines how many prospects, interviews, recruits, FNAs/Internal Consumption, Associates, RMDs it will take.

4. Determines the **time and resources** it will take and what things must be eliminated/sacrificed.

5. Sets daily, weekly, monthly, yearly and multi-year **deadlines** to accomplish the goals.

6. Develops a written **Business Plan** to:

   a. Recruit/train/develop new people.

   b. Have enough personal **sales,** training sales and new **recruits** to keep your personal activity at a high level while building your team/business.

LEADERSHIP FORMAT SYSTEM
RECRUITING & BUILDING FACTORY

DELIVERY SYSTEM TRANSPORTATION

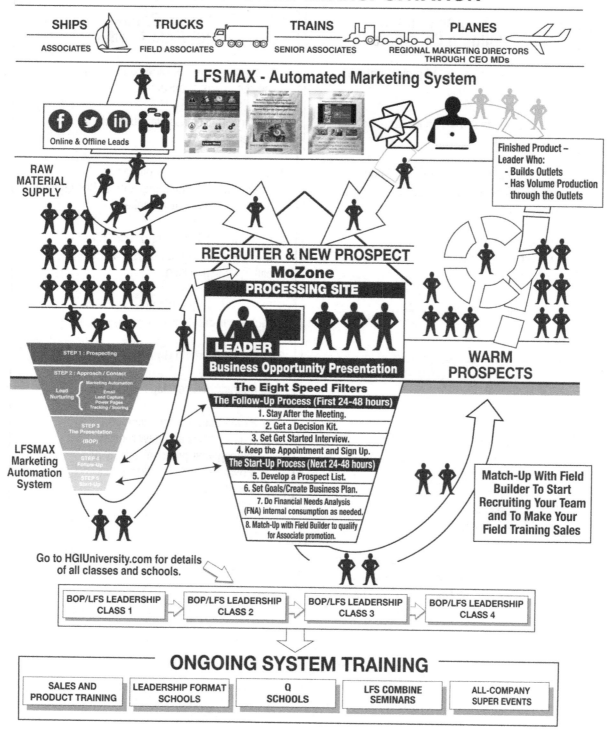

SHIPS	TRUCKS	TRAINS	PLANES
ASSOCIATES	FIELD ASSOCIATES	SENIOR ASSOCIATES	REGIONAL MARKETING DIRECTORS THROUGH CEO MDs

LFSMAX - Automated Marketing System

Online & Offline Leads

RAW MATERIAL SUPPLY

Finished Product –
Leader Who:
- Builds Outlets
- Has Volume Production through the Outlets

RECRUITER & NEW PROSPECT

MoZone
PROCESSING SITE

LEADER
Business Opportunity Presentation

WARM PROSPECTS

STEP 1 : Prospecting

STEP 2 : Approach / Contact

Lead Nurturing
- Marketing Automation
- Email
- Lead Capture
- Power Pages
- Tracking / Scoring

STEP 3 The Presentation (BOP)

LFSMAX Marketing Automation System

STEP 4 Follow-Up

STEP 5 Start-Up

The Eight Speed Filters
The Follow-Up Process (First 24-48 hours)
1. Stay After the Meeting.
2. Get a Decision Kit.
3. Set Get Started Interview.
4. Keep the Appointment and Sign Up.
The Start-Up Process (Next 24-48 hours)
5. Develop a Prospect List.
6. Set Goals/Create Business Plan.
7. Do Financial Needs Analysis (FNA) internal consumption as needed.
8. Match-Up with Field Builder to qualify for Associate promotion.

Match-Up With Field Builder To Start Recruiting Your Team and To Make Your Field Training Sales

Go to HGIUniversity.com for details of all classes and schools.

BOP/LFS LEADERSHIP CLASS 1	BOP/LFS LEADERSHIP CLASS 2	BOP/LFS LEADERSHIP CLASS 3	BOP/LFS LEADERSHIP CLASS 4

ONGOING SYSTEM TRAINING

SALES AND PRODUCT TRAINING	LEADERSHIP FORMAT SCHOOLS	Q SCHOOLS	LFS COMBINE SEMINARS	ALL-COMPANY SUPER EVENTS

The Campaign
of Great Growth

*Execute the Plan to Focus by Using the
Magic of 90-Day Madman Cycles to
Orchestrate Explosive Quantum Growth.*

LINK 4 90-DAY MADMAN CYCLES CONCURRENTLY

GET YOUR GENIE OUT OF YOUR LAMP

PLAN TO FOCUS

10 15 25	
35 50 50	
50 75 75	
100 100 100	

The Magic of
90-Day Madman Cycles

HGI
HEGEMON GROUP INTERNATIONAL

Tip of the Spear
A Plan to Focus — Pathway to CEO MD

	Recruit Guideline	Goal	Actual Result
Month 1	10		
Month 2	15		
Month 3	25		
Month 4	35		
Month 5	50		
Month 6	50		
Month 7	50		
Month 8	75		
Month 9	75		
Month 10	100		
Month 11	100		
Month 12	100		

(Month 10–12: Final Battle)

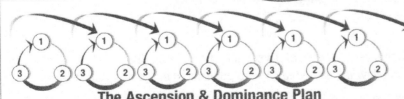

**The Ascension & Dominance Plan
Six 90-Day Madman Cycles**

Section II — BUILDERS MINDSET

The Magic of 90-Day Madman Cycles

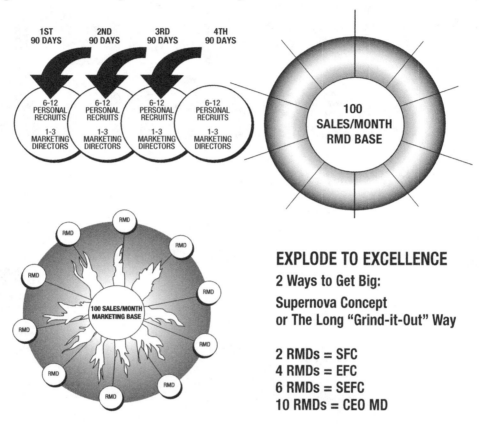

EXPLODE TO EXCELLENCE

2 Ways to Get Big:

**Supernova Concept
or The Long "Grind-it-Out" Way**

**2 RMDs = SFC
4 RMDs = EFC
6 RMDs = SEFC
10 RMDs = CEO MD**

Top Priority

No. 1. The "continuous opening of outlets"

No. 2. Volume production per outlet

In this business, every person is an outlet. YOU are an outlet. An outlet is anyone who can offer the product to the consumer. The difference between this business and other marketing systems is that as an independent contractor, YOU have the ability to set up your own distribution system within the big network.

The Magic of Duplication

Hubert Humphrey has followed the same system for years. This is the same system that most of his successful Leaders adopted. All recruits joining HGI should follow the same blueprint to duplicate their great success.

The best way to get a high level of performance is to be sure that the master copy is worth duplicating.

90-Day Madman Cycles

The whole secret of Hubert Humphrey's success has been the continuous linking together of 90-Day Madman Cycles. In the process, many great super team leaders have been able to duplicate this type of recruiting explosion and produce leaders who do their own Madman Cycles.

The key to unlocking the Plan to Focus is harnessing the Law of Averages by applying the Law of High Numbers during each month of the 90-Day Madman Cycles. Then link 4 CONCURRENT 90-Day Madman Cycles together to orchestrate your team's Campaign of Great Growth.

Key areas of the Plan to Focus:

1. Control Prospect List Development

- Minimum 25 referrals with each membership agreement

- Minimum 10 referrals from each client

- Help every new recruit develop minimum 100 name prospect list

2. Be Contact-Focused

- Leader controls the point of contact/approach

- Leader and new associate act as joint inviters

3. Make the BOP the Heart of your Growth Campaign

- Allows experienced leaders to show the HGI opportunity to prospects

- MoZone at Center converts the prospect

4. Be Follow-Up Intensive

- Conduct the Hiring Interview within 24 to 48 hours

- Rapidly guide the new associate through the 8 Speed Filters

5. Concentrate Every New Associate on Getting Off to a Fast Start

- Begin at Step One

- Leader and new associate begin contact process together within 24 to 48 hours

6. Become a Master Duplicator/Replicator

- Repeat the HGI LFS Success Cycles over and over again

The Magic of Compound Recruiting

The Magic Of Multiples					
		Each Recruit 2	Difference of ONE		Each Recruit 3
Level 1 _____		2 x2	_____		3 x3
Level 2 _____		4 x2	_____		9 x3
Level 3 _____		8 x2	_____		27 x3
Level 4 _____		16 x2	_____		81 x3
Level 5 _____		32 x2	_____		243 x3
Level 6 _____		64 x2	_____		729 x3
Level 7 _____		128 x2	_____		2,187 x3
Level 8 _____		256 x2	_____		6,561 x3
Level 9 _____		512 x2	_____		19,683 x3
		1,024	Difference of 58,025		59,049

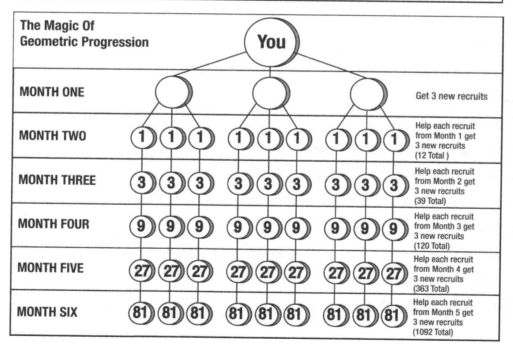

The Magic Of Geometric Progression

You

MONTH ONE — Get 3 new recruits

MONTH TWO — (1)(1)(1) (1)(1)(1) (1)(1)(1) — Help each recruit from Month 1 get 3 new recruits (12 Total)

MONTH THREE — (3)(3)(3) (3)(3)(3) (3)(3)(3) — Help each recruit from Month 2 get 3 new recruits (39 Total)

MONTH FOUR — (9)(9)(9) (9)(9)(9) (9)(9)(9) — Help each recruit from Month 3 get 3 new recruits (120 Total)

MONTH FIVE — (27)(27)(27) (27)(27)(27) (27)(27)(27) — Help each recruit from Month 4 get 3 new recruits (363 Total)

MONTH SIX — (81)(81)(81) (81)(81)(81) (81)(81)(81) — Help each recruit from Month 5 get 3 new recruits (1092 Total)

This is a hypothetical scenario for illustrative purposes only. There is no assurance that these results can or will be achieved.

For training and educational purposes only. Not to be used with the public.

112

The Ultimate Possibility Projection

"Tons of People to BOPs...!!!"

HGI
HEGEMON GROUP INTERNATIONAL

Use the Magic of Multiples to send your RMD Factories into orbit!
Start with <u>THREE</u>, who bring <u>THREE</u>, who bring <u>THREE</u>, etc. and watch the explosion!

MONDAY	TUESDAY	WEDNESDAY	THURSDAY	FRIDAY	SATURDAY	TOTAL
Follow-Up	BOP	Follow-Up	BOP	Follow-Up	BOP	
Find 3 prospects for next BOP (1)*	**3**	(1) BRING 3 → **3**	(3) BRING 3 → **9**	**9**	(9) BRING 3 → **27**	**39** (13)
(9) BRING 3 → **27**	(27) BRING 3 → **81**	**81**	(81) BRING 3 → **243**	**243**	(243) BRING 3 → **729**	**1,092** (364)
(243) BRING 3 → **729**	(729) BRING 3 → **2,187**	**2,187**	(2,187) BRING 3 → **6,561**	**6,561**	(6,561) BRING 3 → **19,683**	**29,523** (9,841)*

*(worst case scenario starting with one)

Imagine the possibilities – even if you spread this out over 3 months, or only achieve 10-20% of these numbers.

For training and educational purposes only. Not to be used with the public.

Tip of the Spear

A Plan to Focus — Pathway to CEO MD

	Recruit Guideline	Goal	Actual Result
MONTH 1	10		
MONTH 2	15		
MONTH 3	25		
MONTH 4	35		
MONTH 5	50		
MONTH 6	50		
MONTH 7	50		
MONTH 8	75		
MONTH 9	75		
MONTH 10	100		
MONTH 11	100		
MONTH 12	100		

FINAL BATTLE (Months 9–12)

Tip of The Spear
A Plan to Focus • Pathway to CEO MD

Leader	/	/	/	/	/	/	/	/	/	/	/	/	/	/	/
Monthly Target															
Monthly Target															
Monthly Target															
Monthly Target															
Monthly Target															
Monthly Target															
Monthly Target															
Monthly Target															
Monthly Target															

Section II — BUILDERS MINDSET

Wealth Builder Challenge
Pin Accountability Chart

PV/Mo. Base _____ PV
(min. 5K/Mo. Base)

PV/Mo. Base _____ PV
(min. 25K/Mo. Base)

LEG 1	LEG 2	LEG 3	LEG 4	LEG 5
1 DEEP	1 DEEP	1 DEEP		1 DEEP
2 DEEP	2 DEEP	2 DEEP	1 DEEP	2 DEEP
3 DEEP	3 DEEP	3 DEEP		3 DEEP
4 DEEP	4 DEEP	4 DEEP	2 DEEP	4 DEEP

PV/Mo. Base _____ PV
(min. 100K/Mo. Base)

PV/Mo. Super Base _____ PV
(min. 250K/Mo. Super Base)

LEG 11	LEG 12	LEG 13	LEG 14	LEG 15
1 DEEP	1 DEEP	1 DEEP	1 DEEP	1 DEEP
2 DEEP	2 DEEP	2 DEEP	2 DEEP	2 DEEP
3 DEEP	3 DEEP	3 DEEP	3 DEEP	3 DEEP
4 DEEP	4 DEEP	4 DEEP	4 DEEP	4 DEEP

LEG 21	LEG 22	LEG 23	LEG 24	LEG 25
1 DEEP	1 DEEP	1 DEEP		1 DEEP
2 DEEP	2 DEEP	2 DEEP	1 DEEP	2 DEEP
3 DEEP	3 DEEP	3 DEEP		3 DEEP
4 DEEP	4 DEEP	4 DEEP	2 DEEP	4 DEEP

Wealth Builder Challenge
Pin Accountability Chart

PV/Mo. Base _____ PV
(min. 50K/Mo. Base)

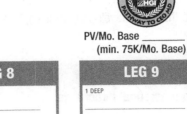

PV/Mo. Base _____ PV
(min. 75K/Mo. Base)

LEG 6	LEG 7	LEG 8	LEG 9	LEG 10
1 DEEP	1 DEEP	1 DEEP	1 DEEP	1 DEEP
2 DEEP	2 DEEP	2 DEEP	2 DEEP	2 DEEP
3 DEEP	3 DEEP	3 DEEP	3 DEEP	3 DEEP
4 DEEP	4 DEEP	4 DEEP	4 DEEP	4 DEEP

PV/Mo. Super Base _____ PV
(min. 500K/Mo. Super Base)

LEG 16	LEG 17	LEG 18	LEG 19	LEG 20
1 DEEP	1 DEEP	1 DEEP	1 DEEP	1 DEEP
2 DEEP	2 DEEP	2 DEEP	2 DEEP	2 DEEP
3 DEEP	3 DEEP	3 DEEP	3 DEEP	3 DEEP
4 DEEP	4 DEEP	4 DEEP	4 DEEP	4 DEEP

PV/Mo. Super Base _____ PV
(min. 1,000,000/Mo. Super Base)

LEG 26	LEG 27	LEG 28	LEG 29	LEG 30
1 DEEP	1 DEEP	1 DEEP	1 DEEP	1 DEEP
2 DEEP	2 DEEP	2 DEEP	2 DEEP	2 DEEP
3 DEEP	3 DEEP	3 DEEP	3 DEEP	3 DEEP
4 DEEP	4 DEEP	4 DEEP	4 DEEP	4 DEEP

Section II — BUILDERS MINDSET

For training and educational purposes only. Not to be used with the public.

Hubert's Two Main Recruiting Focal Points

Hubert has always said that if he developed amnesia, he would want to remember two things in order to build a great team:

1. **Get more and more personal direct legs.**

   - Speed Width

   - Go wide fast.

   - Personally recruit 3-6 new direct legs every 90-day Madman Cycle

   - 60 Wide in 6 Months

   - Width = Profitability

   - To become independently wealthy, develop 7-10 powerful direct Super Team Builders.

2. **Get more and more people (old and new) to BOPs.**

   - See more people faster.

   - 3 main purposes of a BOP:

     — Resell the dream to existing teammates.

     — Teach existing teammates to sell the dream.

     — Sell the dream to new guests.

   - Expose them to the power of MoZone.

   - The "Hold a Meeting" system

   - HGI Proven Success Formula:
     Average No. of people at BOP = Average number of Base Shop Sales per Month

   - The leaders with the most people in high-powered BOPs ultimately make the most money.

The Psychology of Hubert's Building System

1. Remember Two Things:

— You will be paid to imitate, not create.
— Marketing is the creation of the outlet and the movement of product simultaneously.

2. Set Up A System Whereby Recruiting Never Stops

3. Law of High Numbers Makes Law of Averages Profitable

4. Lots of People Doing a Little Bit and a Few Doing a Lot = Success

5. Speed Width (Go Wide Fast)

6. Recruit in Waves (3-12 Wide Every 30 Days)

7. Magic of Dud Power

— Leader with most "duds" wins
— Also will have most successful associates

8. Our Sensitive "Sell The Dream" Machinery Runs On:

— High-octane motivation
— "Hold-a-meeting" commitment

9. Compress Activity/Collapse Time Frames

— Use short 3-4 day blitzes with part-timers.
— Run concurrent 90-Day Madman Cycles.

10. Surge... Explode... Plateau...

— Surge - compress activity (BOP invitations, recruits, etc.)/collapse time frames (use the magic of the 30-day blitz).
— Explode - have an explosion of new recruits, new leaders, new promotions, plus record production and cash flow; seize the momentum while it's on your side.
— Plateau - regroup, re-energize and re-focus to start the cycle all over again.

11. Constant Personal Communication

— Master the art of motivation.
— Great builders set goals for themselves and their people.

12. You Are Always Either:
— Growing
— Dying

13. Two Marketing Focal Points:

— The continuous opening of outlets
— Volume production per outlet

For training and educational purposes only. Not to be used with the public.

The Psychology of Hubert's Building System *(Continued)*

14. Aggressiveness Is Essential To Be A Super Team Builder

Without aggressiveness, all your other capabilities are useless.

Develop The "Firing Habit"

The U.S. Army reports that the No.1 reason 90% of all soldiers never fire a weapon in combat is the lack of confidence in their ability and their weapons.

You need to teach "Drill for Skill" and "Drill for Will" to build confidence within your team.

15. Two Important Minimum Standards of Excellence:

— Average Recruits/RMD Base Shop = 25 new associates/month.
— Average BV/RMD Base Shop = 50-60,000 BV/Mo.

16. Promotions Drive Production

— Harness each new recruit to hit Senior Associate by producing 3 strong legs.
— Harness each Senior Associate to hit RMD by producing 3 consecutive big production months.
— Harness each RMD to EFC by producing 6 direct RMDs.
— Harness each EFC to SEFC by producing 9 qualified direct RMDs.
— Harness each SEFC to CEO MD by producing 15 qualified direct RMDs.

17. Build Big Production Teams That Produce Big Income

— Build $25,000/Yr. Earners
— Build $50,000 Earners
— Build $100,000 (6-Figure Earners)
— Build $250,000 Earners
— Build $500,000 Earners
— Build $1,000,000 (7-Figure Earners)
— Build $10,000,000 (8-Figure Earners)

For training and educational purposes only. Not to be used with the public.

120

The Psychology of Hubert's Building System *(Continued)*

18. Success Cycle

"Max-Out" Success Cycle	"Average" Success Cycle
Attitude Drives Prospecting	Product Focus Drives Sales
Prospecting Drives Recruiting	Sales Drive Average Production
Recruiting Drives Promotions	Average Production Drives Average Promotions
Promotions Drive Production	Average Promotions Build Average Managers
Production Drives Earnings	Average Managers Earn Average Cash Flow
Earnings Drive Wealth	Average Cash Flow Drives an Average Career
Wealth Drives Leadership	Average Career Drives an Average Lifestyle

19. "Carpe Diem" – Seize the Day!

20. Become A Legend of the Future

The battle cry of all New Era HGI Leaders should be ASCENSION and DOMINANCE.
For those who are RELENTLESS in COPYING and DOING EXACTLY what the SUPERSTARS OF
THE PAST did, it is INEVITABLE that they will become the LEGENDS OF THE FUTURE.

21. The Fastest way to become a MILLIONAIRE…
Find one… Then do EXACTLY what he/she does.

22. The Greatest Motivation Comes From:

— Self-confidence
— Self-esteem
— Know-how
— A system of accountability
— Repetition – "Relentless Inevitability"
— A plan that works

Who Motivates the Motivator?

— The key: The motivator himself.

23. You Should Also Have a Socrates/Plato Relationship

24. Thermostat vs. Thermometer:

— **Thermometer people** – These are controlled by outside circumstances. If everyone around them is "hot," they're "hot." If everyone around them is "cold," they're "cold."
— **Thermostat people** – These people set their "temperature" in advance. Rather than just adjust to the "temperature" of other people, they cause other people to adjust to their pre-determined "excitement level!" They don't let others drag them down. They pull the others UP!!

The Psychology of Hubert's Building System *(Continued)*

25. Stop Recruiting People to a Business

Recruit them to the environment. Let the atmosphere of the office, BOP or Leadership Format School recruit them.

26. Change Your Paradigms

27. Be a Student of the Business.

— Knowledge does not produce activity.
— Activity produces knowledge.
— Repetition is the mother of skill.

28. Constant Course Correction

Apollo 11 was off course 90% of the time, but landed on the moon. Expect adversity and use it to achieve your mission.

29. To Achieve Greatness You Must:

— Think strategically
— Commit specifically
— Focus constantly

30. Success Will Always Revolve Around These 3 Steps:

— Focus
— Motivation
— Execution

31. Definiteness of Purpose:

— Decisiveness
— Persistence

32. Great Leaders Must Focus On:

— Stretching Vision/Then Motivate
— Big Events/Great Events
— Big Leaders/Great Leaders
— Big Things/Great Things

The Psychology of Hubert's Building System *(Continued)*

33. Seize Their Imagination/Fuel Their Dreams

34. Press On

Nothing in the world can take the place of persistence. Talent will not. Nothing is more common than unsuccessful men with talent. Genius will not. Unrewarded genius is almost a proverb. Education alone will not. The world is full of educated derelicts. PERSISTENCE and DETERMINATION ALONE are OMNIPOTENT.

35. Recruit to Build vs. Recruit to Sell

36. Example of Growing Grass or Killing Weeds

37. The Habit of Persistence from Think and Grow Rich
   Use these four steps to develop persistence:

   — A definite purpose backed by a burning desire for its fulfillment
   — A definite plan, expressed in continuous action
   — A mind closed tightly against all negative and discouraging influences, including
      negative suggestions of relatives, friends and acquaintances
   — A friendly alliance with one or more persons who will encourage one to follow
      through with both plan and purpose

38. Mastermind Alliance

   Batteries hooked up in series are stronger than any one battery.

39. Keep the Main Thing the Main Thing

40. Three Obstacles to Spontaneous Recruiting:

   — Leaders don't sell the big-time opportunity of having large multiples of people to override.
   — First emphasis with a new recruit is to "Field Train" vs. "Get him/her 3 new recruits."
   — They focus on possibly making $1,000 or more on a sale vs. getting a recruit decision first.

41. Focus on Recruiting and Sales Will Come

   — Aim at recruits/Hit sales.
   — Sell to those you recruit/Sell to those you don't recruit.

The Psychology of Hubert's Building System *(Continued)*

42. Develop a Recruiter's Mentality:

— Approach every prospect about the opportunity first.
— Hold off on the client data/sale until you have their recruit decision.
— Sell the Dream and the Crusade simultaneously.
— Infect enthusiasm and inject crusading fervor.
— Focus on recruiting and sales will come
— Aim at recruits/Hit sales.
— Sell to those you recruit/Sell to those you don't recruit.
— Be Like a Quarterback:
  • Every play is planned to be a touchdown bomb. (Recruit the prospect.)
  • If defense is stacked against this, call an audible to check off.
  • Hand off to running back to at least gain 3-4 yards (Get data/Make sale).

43. People Have Always Been Intrigued by Multiples and Geometric Progression:

— Show them how to build using the multiples.
— A picture is worth a thousand words.

44. Ladder of Evolution

From…

— Nobody to Upstart
— Upstart to Contender
— Contender to Winner
— Winner to Champion
— Champion to Dynasty

45. A Mission That Motivates

— HGI's mission is to produce more financially independent people
  ($100,000/year-$1,000,000/year earners) than any other business in history.

46. Multiplex Income

— "Sales Management" or "Team Building"
— Allows large unlimited income, based on your effort and abilities, through building and overriding an organization
— Allows security through having many people's time working toward your benefit
— Self-replicating, self-motivated, self-financed

No. of People	No. of Hours
1	24 per day
10	240 per day
100	2,400 per day
1000	24,000 per day

The Psychology of Hubert's Building System *(Continued)*

47. Discipline and Accountability Leads to Ascension and Dominance.

48. You Are What You Repeatedly Do. Excellence is not an Act, But a Habit.

— Sow a thought…reap an action…
— Sow an action…reap a habit…
— Sow a habit…reap a character…
— Sow a character…reap a destiny…

49. Use the "Controlled Ignorance" Formula:

— "Stumble forward and stay confused."
— Capitalize on the excitement of your new recruits' "Ignorant Enthusiasm."
— You must always have a pioneer attitude and spirit.
— Constantly stay alert for people to recruit.

50. Have a Relentless Inevitability:

"Take away my factories, my plants; take away my railroads, my ships, my transportation; take away my money; strip me of all of these, but leave me my men, and in two or three years I will have them all again."
— Andrew Carnegie

"Give me 10 driven determined dreamers and soon I'll give you 100,000 more."
— Hubert Humphrey

The Psychology of Hubert's Building System *(Continued)*

Time-Tested Absolutes:

— Aim at recruiting prospect up front 100% of the time.

— Immediately aim at recruiting a new recruit's prospects up front 100% of the time.

— You must strive to become a Building Contractor (Leader/Builder) not just a Carpenter (Product Salesperson).

— Quit quitting and stop stopping – this will contribute to you beating 95% of your competitors (Keep the pipeline full).

— Duplicate/transfer leadership techniques to key people at all levels to perpetuate growth – always drive your leadership deeper and deeper.

— Get new recruits off to a fast start within the first 24 to 48 hours – just like a new baby their first 2-3 days of life are their most critical.

— Develop a recruiting rhythm

— Your leaders need to hold BOPs at least one night a week, preferably three.

— Teach yourself and your people to use the experience and resources of their upline leadership team.

— Don't re-invent the wheel. Remember, you are paid to imitate, not create.

— Recruiting large numbers in short periods creates momentum.

— Leaders with momentum on their side will WIN.

— Recruiting isn't the key to our business, it is our business.

— Don't be scared to recruit upward. Recruit your equal or better and your team will always improve.

— All great leaders are great followers.

The Power of the RMD Position

"HGI challenges all entrepreneurial-minded people to come form an alliance with us, and build to the RMD level to conquer their futures."

> — Hubert Humphrey
> HGI Founder and Architect of the System

The HGI Regional Marketing Director contract is the ultimate contract in business.

– You don't have to buy it.

– You don't play politics and climb the corporate ladder to get there.

– You just have to earn it.

– There are an unlimited number of positions available.

– You can start your own business with ...

- No big start-up costs

- No job risk

- No product inventory required

- No franchise fees

- No experience required

HGI allows you to be in business for yourself, but not by yourself. You run the system. The system runs the business. The system is what allows you to have a great quality of life. The HGI Leadership Format System is proven, predictable, foolproof and profitable. Our mentors will help you duplicate yourself over and over again.

The two main purposes of a strong RMD Base:

No. 1 – Provides tremendous financial rewards through powerful override spread

No. 2 – Runs an RMD Factory, the source of all future leadership and sets the example for your team

Running the RMD Factory

Two Main Focal Points:

- Continuous opening of outlets
- Continuous volume production through the outlets

Two levels of the RMD Factory:

1. "System whereby recruiting never stops."
2. "System whereby promoting new RMDs never stops."

The No. 1 challenge to great growth:

RMD promotion speed must equal recruiting speed.

RMD promotions show that your RMD Factory works.

The prospects are the raw material RMDs are the finished product.

All great builders construct RMD hierarchies.

Promote the power of the RMD position. Lay out the profile from birth.

Leadership Role

The only way to build a lasting empire is by perpetually building strong RMDs, which requires strong leadership.

- You have the responsibility to master the Leadership Format System and teach your teammates the best way to maximize the HGI opportunity by running the Pure System.

- You must lead from the front by being a "Do-it-first" leader.

- You must always lead by example.

- You must become a Director of Motivation — travel, hold big events, recognize your leaders, start a team newsletter, etc.

- You must perpetually build big Base Shops.

- You must continually produce RMDs from your RMD Factory Base Shop.

Running the RMD Factory

"It is impossible for a leader to build a huge hierarchy and not maintain a strong RMD base shop. It is the key to your success in HGI. There is no other area as critical to your long-range success."

— Hubert Humphrey, HGI Founder & Architect of the System

7 Reasons Why You Must Build a Strong RMD Base Shop

1. It gives you leadership power with your people who will believe in and follow you because of your example.

- You must build and maintain the prototype for your RMDs to duplicate. They must physically be able to come to your center and see a perfectly running LFS model.

- You show your leadership prowess by competing on the Leaders Bulletins in all categories, including personal and base shop. (People don't want to follow a team builder who "used to do it.")

2. It is your main source of income and profitability until you build a big, strong, national Infinity Team.

- You should never count on RMD overrides until you consistently cash flow $10,000 each month from your base shop and personal production from Field Building.

- Your base shop is where your biggest spreads always come from.

3. You will not lose touch with your leaders.

- By staying in the trenches, you're not just teaching the system, you're living it.

- It keeps you fresh and new in the business – each new recruit re-energizes you again about the HGI opportunity.

- It's the starting point for building strong personal relationships as your base shop associates become your new front-line leaders.

4. You will not lose your mental toughness.

- It requires work to build and run an RMD base shop. It keeps you focused and strong in fundamentals.

- You will NEVER lose the skills that make the difference in winning and losing.

Running the RMD Factory *(Continued)*

5. You can be the example for your people.

- By running a strong, successful RMD base shop, you take all the excuses away from your leaders.

When your leaders say...	YOU can say...
"Nobody's recruiting…"	(MY base shop is.)
"Nobody's selling…"	(MY base shop is.)
"I'm not making any money…"	(I am.)
"I can't run a base shop and work with RMDs too…"	(I do.)

6. The base shop is where the action is.

- All activity begins and ends in the RMD base shop.

- Your RMD base shop should be the hub of your entire team.

- When the leader is in the hunt and highly involved everyday, he/she can help keep leaders moving forward in the business, and keep them up and positive.

7. A successful base shop demands a positive attitude.

- If the attitude and atmosphere of your base shop is explosive and exciting, your activity and activity of your leaders will be explosive and exciting.

- You must be excited, positive, and have the right attitude 100% of the time.

- You must make sure your people have the same attitude as well.

- If you maintain a positive attitude, you will be successful and happy in all areas of your life.

For training and educational purposes only. Not to be used with the public.

130

Running the RMD Factory *(Continued)*

How to Lead your RMD Factory from a Local Start-up Operation to National Superstar Status

- You can't make excuses when you're playing bad. You have to make corrections, no alibis.

- Never let your people down. Commit to be there to help lead them through the tough times.

- It should never be too tough for you – it was common for Hubert to travel 5,000 miles in one week during his field era.

- As the leader, you can't have a bad day. Everybody is counting on you.

- When you get to a meeting, the light must turn on!

- Super team leaders must be as fresh today as they were when they joined the company.

- You must be the hardest working, most energized leader on your team.

- The business must be fun. Work hard, play hard.

- Don't let the money change you. Remember where you came from and stay true to yourself.

- Not everybody on your team will like you and you won't necessarily like everybody on your team, but they should never know it. (You always should love them all, even if you don't like something about them.)

- You need to have the toughest hide in the business.

- It's not where you are from, or where you are, but where you're going that counts.

- Be driven by one-third enjoyment and love, one-third ego, and one-third financial.

- You must never be satisfied!

- You should want to prove to yourself you can get better every year!

The Magic of Compound Recruiting

HUBERT HUMPHREY'S CORE GROUP OF LEADERS

RMD-type
EFC-type
SEFC-type

THIS IS A POWERFUL PICTURE SHOWING THE MASSIVE EXPANSE OF HUBERT'S LEADERSHIP TEAM THAT, AT ITS PEAK IN 1989 DURING HIS ALW FIELD ERA, LED A TEAM OF 50,000.

Hubert's Career Best Effort

In His Field Leader Era

In the quest to set new records for your Career Best Effort, the new you must always beat the old you. Now, Hubert Humphrey issues the ultimate challenge – beat his Career Best Effort.

Hubert's Record-Breaking Personal Earnings

	ACTUAL FIELD INCOME	PROJECTED INCOME WITH TODAY'S PRODUCT LINES
1978	$105,000	$693,000
1979	$375,000	$2,475,000
1980	$650,000	$4,290,000
1981	$1,100,000	$7,260,000
1982	$1,600,000	$10,560,000
1983	$1,900,000	$12,540,000
1984	$2,300,000	$15,180,000
1985	$2,800,000	$18,480,000
1986	$3,100,000	$20,460,000
1987	$3,300,000	$21,780,000
1988	$3,500,000	$23,100,000
1989	$3,700,000	$24,420,000
1990	$3,900,000	$25,740,000
1991	$3,900,000	$25,740,000
Total	**$33,700,000**	**$222,420,000**

FOR EDUCATIONAL AND TRAINING PURPOSES ONLY.

Hubert's Record-Breaking Recruiting and Production

Total Team Size	400,000 Recruits 50,000 Insurance-Licensed Associates 7,800 Dually Licensed Associates
Total RMD Base Shop Size	2,000 Licensed Associates
Total RMD Base Shop Production (In One Month)	2,000 Life Sales/Mo. 4,000,000 PV/Mo.
Total Infinity Team Production (In One Month)	20,000 Life Sales/Mo. 30,000,000 PV/Mo.
Total RMD Base Shop Recruits (In One Month)	595 Recruits/Mo.
Total Infinity Team Recruits (In One Month)	8,000 Recruits/Mo.
Total 1st Gen. RMDs	120 RMDs
Total Infinity Team RMDs	6,000 RMDs
Total Infinity Team Sales (In One Year)	300,000 Sales/Yr. 150,000,000 Premium/Yr.
Total Personal Commission Cash Flow in 14-year Career	$33,700,700
Total $100,000 Ring Earners	500+ Leaders

FOR EDUCATIONAL AND TRAINING PURPOSES ONLY.

Section II — BUILDERS MINDSET

Build Leaders and Teams Will Come

- It all starts with building leaders.
- HGI must convert...
    - Personal Producers into Leaders...
    - Managers into Leaders...
    - Recruiters into Leaders...
    - Executives into Leaders.
- All great leaders were, and still are, great followers.
- In order to be a master replicator, you must first be a master duplicator.
- Be a Do-It-First Leader, a master copy worth duplicating.
- Learn how to identify leaders early by their passion, will to win and work ethic.
- Allow them to grow in their leadership role, or you will run into the Law of Diminishing Returns.
- Make your dreams come true by creating a lasting business built on strong leaders.

Exposing the Myths of Leadership

- Leadership is not a birthright. It must be earned.
- Do-It-First Leadership will always be your No. 1 responsibility, long after your initial success.
- Leadership is the No. 1 reason you are paid overrides.

Two Most Critical Challenges Facing All Leaders

1. Build a Big Business

- 100% Commitment to Quantity
- Be a student and teacher of the Leadership Format System.
- Commit to and run a system whereby...
    - Prospect List development...never stops!
    - Invitations...never stop!
    - Recruiting...never stops!

For training and educational purposes only. Not to be used with the public.

134

Build A Big Business *(Continued)*

- Building…never stops!
- Promotions…never stop!
- High-Volume Production…never stops!
- Creation of big-time Money-Making Leaders…never stops!
- Duplication…never stops!
- Get more personal direct legs.
- Get more and more people – old and new – to BOPs.
- Harness the power of 90-day Madman Cycles.
- Put the Law of High Numbers and the Law of Averages to work for you.
- Have a "Fast-Start Mentality."
- Run the Hero-Making Machine
- Get all leaders on track with a motivational focus:
  - HGI Achievement System – Fight for your next promotion.
  - HGI Wealth Builder Circle – Earn Success Society watches and Champion's Club rings.
- Tap into "Magic of the Multiples" that has created millions for so many.

2. **Run a Big Business**

- 100% Commitment to Quality.
- Be a student and teacher of high-quality production through your outlets.
- High Numbers Mentality.
- Commit to and run a system whereby…
  - Recruiting in the Right Markets…never stops!
  - Quality Product Training…never stops!
  - Training on 3 Field Training Sales with an experienced field leader…never stops!
  - The HGI 3-Step Sales Process…never stops!
- Conquer through Quality.

Run A Big Business *(Continued)*

- Conquer through proper supervision.
- Make decisions thinking as an owner.
- Lead by Example.

    - Be the Best Recruiter, Prospector, Closer, Trainer, etc.
    - Make Big Money.
    - Build Big & Strong Base Shop.
    - Build Minimum 7 to 10 Strong 1st-Generation RMDs.

"To the leaders who build a big Base Shop and keep producing 1st-generation RMDs go the greatest honors and greatest rewards."

— Hubert Humphrey
HGI Founder & Architect of the System

HGI Standards of Excellence

The following is a profile that all HGI Leaders must hold themselves up against to be considered a World Class Super Team Builder/Leader.

	Poor	Fair	Good	Excellent
Personal *				
Recruits	1	3	7	10
No. of Sales/BV	1/4,000	5/20,000	10/40,000	25/100,000
RMD Base				
Recruits	5	10	50	100
No. of Sales/BV	5/20,000	25/100,000	100/400,000	250/1,000,000
Super Base				
Recruits	15	50	150	300
No. of Sales/BV	15/60,000	75/300,000	200/800,000	500/2,000,000
Super Team				
Recruits	30	100	1,000	3,000
No. of Sales/BV	50/200,000	250/1,000,000	500/4,000,000	2,500/10,000,000
Cash Flow	under			
	$ 50,000	$ 100,000	$ 500,000	$ 1,000,000

From Possibility Thinker to Impossibility Achiever

10 Keys to Becoming a Great Leader

1. Desire — 212°

You must have a case of "I want to." You've got to put some logs on that fire and you've got to stoke it until it becomes a burning white-heat desire if you're to achieve big-time success. If you don't want it bad enough, you're never going to get it.

You can drive a horse to water, you can't make him drink, but you can salt his oats and make him thirsty. You've got to learn to salt your own oats … and learn to salt the oats of other people.

2. Willingness to Work

It doesn't matter how much desire you have. If you aren't willing to work hard, you're in trouble. You'll always look for short cuts. There are a lot of guys who desire a million dollars but they go rob banks. You've got to be willing to work.

3. Belief

Read the first 36 pages of Think & Grow Rich. Look at page 36, "The Six Steps to Turn your Desire into Goals," especially steps 5 and 6 where you write it out in great detail. Read your goals over and over with vivid imagination, until you fix what you want permanently in your mind — it gives you a clear vision that you can do it.

4. Commitment — 100%

You make the decision that you are going to put out your 100% effort every day. You're going to go through all the "nos" and "yeses," to do this business. The commitment will only come after the belief. It's impossible and goes against nature to expect to make a 100% commitment to something that you don't totally believe in.

5. Repetitious and Systematic — LFS

You must become a student of the business and master the Leadership Format System.

6. Know-How

You must have knowledge. Remember that knowledge does not produce activity...activity produces knowledge.

7. Relentless Inevitability

You must have a relentless inevitability. Through following a system, you become repetitiously predictable and dynamically methodical until you gain experience. Experience is the key to greatness.

8. High F.Q. (Failure Quotient)

A high failure quotient — If you don't have a high failure quotient, you're in trouble. It is not your I.Q., it is your F.Q. What does it take to knock you down? Can you get up one more time than you get knocked down? You have the ability to lovercome obstacles. Like a Timex watch — you've got to take a lickin' and keep on tickin'.

9. Vision

People follow people who are visionary. The scriptures tell us that where there is no vision, the people perish. Lack of vision is one of the biggest obstacles to great leadership.

10. Director of Motivation

You must become a master MOTIVATOR. Leaders do make a difference. When you recruit someone do two things: First share your goals. Let them know they are dealing with a leader who's going someplace. Second, help them set their goals — then help them accomplish them.

Section II — BUILDERS MINDSET

Partners in Business

It is critical to your long-range success that you and your spouse or significant other develop a strong Business Partner relationship.

Business Partners serve as the backbone of your business, your constant source of motivation, inspiration and support. You will never be as big as you want to be without a strong Business Partner.

Unlike most businesses, Hegemon Group International recognizes the spouse as a vital part of the company. As a new Hegemon Group International Business Partner, you are part of the company, and you are invited and encouraged to attend every company function.

Although there are many ways you can help and support your spouse, we believe that "attitude is everything." Being positive during tough times and believing in your spouse is very important. Here are a few other things to keep in mind that can make all the difference:

"When two uncommon people pursue a common dream, it's inevitable that they will achieve uncommon success."

> — *Norma Humphrey*
> *Wife and Business Partner of*
> *HGI Founder & Architect of the System, Hubert Humphrey*

- Be informed about the company and its philosophy. Depend on your upline Business Partner to supply you with company news and information via meetings, newsletters, etc.

- Be proud of what your partner is doing; have faith and trust in your partner's abilities.

- Listen when your partner shares the business with you.

- Give your partner the freedom to succeed.

- Help set goals and be willing to work for them.

- Know that your support makes a difference.

- Attend all Leadership Format Schools, Business Opportunity Presentations and Conventions — you will learn a lot and be able to help your spouse a great deal in the process.

- Get involved with your Business Partner — and stay involved.

One Company...One Product...One System

When the history of HGI is written, our leaders will fall into one of three categories:

— Those who "maximized" the moment, by building great teams.
— Those who "shared" the moment, by focusing only on sales.
— Those who "missed" the moment, by letting it pass them by.

It is critical in this, "The Golden Era of HGI," that you understand that:

— There is one company...Hegemon Group International.
— There is one product...the opportunity.
— There is one system...the Leadership Format System.

Simple Rules For Becoming A Great Leader

1. You must commit to running a system whereby recruiting never stops.

2. Discipline and accountability lead to ascension and dominance.

3. Fight to win. The way to win is never lose.

4. Develop a millionaire's mindset.

5. Be aggressive or all of your other capabilities are wasted.

6. Develop a plan to simplify and multiply. Recruit & motivate. Run a system whereby recruiting and motivation never stop.

7. Commit to excellence.

8. Establish a world-class recognition and reward system for your team.

9. Recruit people to an environment. Stop recruiting them to a business. Let the atmosphere of the office, BOP or Leadership Format School recruit them.

10. Think strategically. Commit specifically. Focus constantly.

11. Success will always revolve around these three steps: Focus. Motivation. Execution.

12. Never lose sight of your No. 1 responsibility: to build leaders.

Churchill, at a pivotal time during World War II, gave two direct orders:

Direct order No. 1 "Organize and succeed at all costs."
Direct order No. 2 "There will be no further orders."

HGI, at a pivotal time as we enter this phase of our company growth, has two direct orders:

Direct order No. 1 "Build Leaders and Teams will come."
Direct order No. 2 "There will be no further orders."

The Keys to Explosive Growth

Recruiting Surge or Explosive Growth

I. "Real Growth" - Focus on Recruits

To dramatically increase the size of your team:
1. Dramatically increase your monthly recruiting speed.
2. Link together four 90-day madman recruiting cycles.
3. Greatly increase number of new recruits that actually get a recruit and that make training sales.
4. Greatly increase number of new associates that get fully W-9 approved and complete FNA.
5. Greatly increase number of new associates that complete Internal Consumption and Field Training Sales.
6. Greatly increase number of new associates that get promotions to Sr. Associate and higher.

II. Growth mentality requires:

1. A massive change of attitude
2. A mighty burst of energy
3. An aggressive vertical move

HIGHER LAW	LESSER LAW
Aim at building leadership teams	Aim at titles
It's how you feel...	...not what you know
Build and direct dynasties	Run a dynasty
Will	Skill
Leader	Manager
Pumping Leadership	Pumping production
King maker	King
TEAM	ME

The HGI Exchange Principles

I. PERSONAL SALE EXCHANGE (I.C. Exchange)

You exchange the right to make your own personal sale for the right to make all personal sales to everyone you ever personally recruit based upon their personal needs.

II. FIELD TRAINING EXCHANGE

You submit yourself to complete the field training program with your leader one time for the right to field train all personal recruits you build in your base shop.

III. PROMOTION QUALIFICATION EXCHANGE

You qualify for all of your promotions up to RMD and above, and in exchange, all of your future RMDs will have to hit their promotions by completing the guidelines as well.

IV. BUILDERS LEG EXCHANGE

You must provide your up-line RMD a strong Builders leg of his/her choice upon your new promotion to RMD. In exchange, you earn the right to take a strong Builders leg exchange from each of the 1st generation RMDs you promote in the future.

The Builders Exchange

The Key to Width and Profitability

One of the keys to the Hubert Humphrey leadership team's success has always been the Builders Exchange. This unique part of the system allows you to maintain a big RMD Base while continuing to promote new RMD leaders. It is the source of tremendous personal width and profitability of your business.

The Traditional Catch-22

One of the biggest challenges facing businesses in our country today is the ability for an individual to move upward in their company based on their efforts or performance. Most end up in a situation where their advancement is hindered because it would be a detriment to their manager or senior leader.

It's a Catch-22: If the person moves up, it's at the expense of the leader, and if they are held back it is at the expense of their own family and personal income.

The Builders Exchange Solves This Problem

Upon promotion to Regional Marketing Director (RMD), the new RMD promotee makes a one-time "exchange" of his or her best leg to the promoting RMD. The Builders Exchange is the choice of the promoting RMD.

The exchange allows the upline promoting RMD to maintain a strong RMD base, while the new RMD increases his or her contract. The new RMD is then in position to receive exchange legs from every new RMD he or she ever produces in the future.

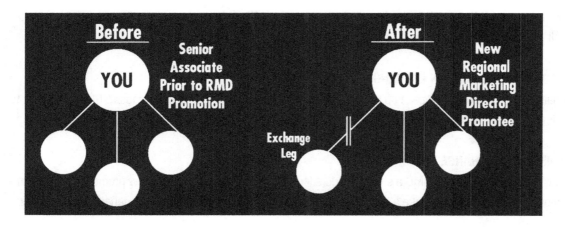

As a senior associate prior to your new RMD promotion, you produce 2 sales/month personally with three (3) field associates who produce 2 sales/month each.

Personal		
$8,000 Field Payout x 60%	=	$4,800
Overrides		
$24,000 Field Payout x 10% (60% - 50%)	=	$2,400
Total Cash Flow		**$7,200**

After your new promotion to RMD, you produce 2 sales/month personally. . . . . . and two (2) field associates produce 2 sales/month each.

Personal		
$8,000 x 80%	=	$6,400
Overrides		
$16,000 x 30% (80% - 50%)	=	$4,800
Total Cash Flow		**$11,200**

HGI leaders promoted to RMD will see immediate benefit from the commission increase, but the real key to the Builders Exchange is the unlimited width that can be generated through this incredible program. You work deep temporarily with your down-line to build permanent front-line width.

When you promoted "A" to RMD and took one of his or her senior associates as a Builders Exchange leg, then, when you promote "B" to RMD, you will be taking "C" and "D," and so on. One direct leader can be transformed into unlimited width, which is one of the biggest keys to running a profitable business.

The Builders Exchange is one of the great uniqueness of HGI's system, which allows you to build and run a big organization. It allows you to maintain a strong RMD base and at the same time continue to spin-out new frontline leaders and allow you to maximize the HGI compensation system while building wide and deep.

To get big, there are two things you must do:

1) The person leaving your RMD base leaves a void. You can identify RMD promotion candidates prior to their promotion so you can build a strong relationship with the RMD's team to help him or her earn the promotion, but also to build a strong Builders Exchange leg in your base.

2) Go on a personal recruiting campaign to recruit new legs to replace your newly-promoted RMD in your base. You should never plan on living on just Builders Exchange legs. Remember, you must maintain the RMD Base master copy to be duplicated by all of your down-line leaders.

The Magic of the Spread for Builders Exchange

You must maintain a strong RMD Base to maximize your profitability. In HGI's revolutionary compensation system, the largest percentage of the total commission package will always be paid at the top:

- Personal
- RMD Base
- RMD Super Base through 1st Gen.

As a leader, you must make sure there is always an upward pull/push of good, dynamic people.

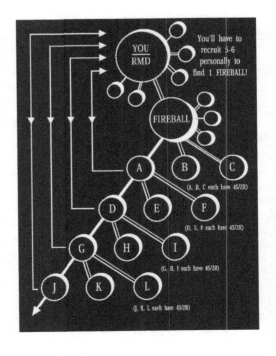

Recurring Revenue from HGI Builders Exchange

RMD has the opportunity to earn recurring revenue from the Leg he/she exchanged. In all previous Builder Exchange opportunities no further income was earned off the exchanged Leg.

1) If you are promoted to a HGI RMD, and you maintain a minimum of 50,000 Business Value (AV) Points per month in your new RMD Base Shop, you will receive 50% of the earnings your upline leader receives from the exchange you provided. Your upline leader who received the exchange Leg would receive 50% of the income.

2) If you are promoted to a HGI RMD, and you maintain a minimum of 25,000 Business Value (AV) Points and up to 49,999 Business Value (AV) Points per month in your new RMD Base Shop, you will receive 25% of the earnings your upline leader receives from the exchange you provided. Your upline leader who received the exchange Leg would receive 75% of the income.

3) If you are promoted to a HGI RMD, and you maintain less than 25,000 Business Value (AV) Points per month in your new RMD Base Shop, you will receive 0% of the earnings your upline leader receives from the exchange you provided. Your upline leader who received the exchange Leg would receive 100% of the income.

Our new system provides both the newly promoted RMD and the RMD making the promotion a great opportunity to grow, work together, and make money together for years to come.

For training and educational purposes only. Not to be used with the public.

144

NOTES:

For training and educational purposes only. Not to be used with the public.

145

NOTES:

A Director of Motivation

Profile of the Great Builders

All the great builders must do more than recruit and train a few people and work downline. They must build wide, and maintain big marketing bases, producing 100,000 to 200,000 BV a month. They must run big BOP systems, and be successful in recruiting and training 100 or more people a month in their Base for several years. They build strong personal relationships with all their key people. They produce giant CEO MD-type teams.

The 10-Point Profile of a Strong RMD:

1. **Attitude**
   Totally positive, loyal to the spirit of the business.

2. **Income**
   Cash flow of $10,000 to $15,000 per month.

3. **Total Business Person**
   A student of the business, manages activity and focuses on results; makes money/saves money.

4. **Quality Business**
   Maintains high levels of compliance and supervision, to ensure quality of business.

5. **Strong Builder**
   Never stops running the leadership factory, continuously builds new waves of leaders.

6. **Business Center**
   Runs a quality office with right facilities for high-powered BOPs and training classes.

7. **Support Staff**
   Hires a sharp administrative team.

8. **Savings**
   Sets aside enough cash to assure at least one year's rent and key business expenses.

9. **Strong Base After Promoting RMDs.**
   Always builds wide and deep.

10. **Motivation/Communication**
    A good leader; good at motivating and communicating downline using the latest in cutting-edge technology.

CPC – Constant Personal Communication

The great legends of the past have always mastered the art of communication to large groups of people at all levels. They worked with every leader as if they were first generation to them. They held big events to give major recognition; they mastered the art of personal letters, newsletters, monthly leaders bulletins and conference calls. They made the commitment to go and visit their leaders locally on a regular basis. They understood that Constant Personal Communication was critical to their success.

To be a legend of the future, you must implement this same type of dynamic communication throughout your team.

Communicate – Communicate – Communicate

There are three types of communication you need to have with your leaders:

- **Constant Personal Motivation**

    Give praise when someone does well. Encourage when someone is "down."

- **Constant Personal Information**

    Everyone loves good news - share it.

- **Constant Personal Education**

    Share recruiting, building and sales techniques. People must have the "know how."

Communication is the key to growing a giant team. You must work to build a giant "irrigation" system so that the information gets to every single person on your team. General Patton's tank army was much more powerful than the traditional foot soldier army, but it presented a whole new set of challenges.

The traditional foot soldier could get by on C rations and water. But the tanks needed fuel and lots of it. They thrived on "high octane," and could not move an inch without it. It was never easy managing the constant delivery of fuel to a moving army, but in the end, it was worth it. The tank army was so powerful it devastated the enemy.

You must make sure your leaders have the high-octane motivation and constant communication they need to build their business.

Constant Personal Motivation

You must plan to communicate almost daily with your key leaders for their first two years. This applies whether they are a thousand miles away or in the same city.

Your leaders need to hear your praise when they do a good job, and your encouragement when they're feeling down. This type of communication can mean everything to your team's success. Your role is to be a vision stretcher, not a problem-solver.

One of the ways to achieve greatness is understanding the importance of setting goals, both short- and long-term. A lot of leaders are capable of setting goals for themselves, but they miss out on a whole other dimension of leadership by failing to set goals for their people.

You must send out "Possibility Projections" on a regular basis. These are projections of how many recruits or how much production each person in your base will do in one month's time. It helps stretch the vision of your team.

A similar method of goal setting is "Promotion Timetables." These are printed projections for the month that a person in your downline team will achieve a certain promotion. For example, have a posted promotion list that includes every one of your leaders. Even if the person doesn't make it, it gives them something specific to shoot for. They have a mental picture of themselves reaching that next level.

Alignment with the HGI Hero-Making Machine

RMDs develop local heroes in their base who get into the gravitational pull of EFC-SEFC leaders who likewise pull those leaders into the gravitational pull of CEO MD leaders who in turn get them into the all-company gravitational pull. You need to have a balance that allows you to attract, nurture and build people from all walks of life and all levels of ambition.

How to Develop Competitive Leaders

- Run a system that reaches people of all levels of commitment to help them achieve their goals and dreams.
- Constantly encourage and inspire them with Constant Personal Communication.
- Recognize associates at all levels, not just your elite leaders.
- Use overlapping leadership to find highly competitive people who are willing to take charge.
- Remember, the key to success in our business is lots of people doing a little, led by a few doing a lot.

How to Develop Highly Competitive Leaders

- Highly competitive leaders do all of the things competitive leaders do and a lot more.
- Define reality to inspire the hard-chargers to have "Career Best Efforts."
- Fuel competition from within your team.
- Challenge people to compete on the monthly leaders bulletin and win all company contests.
- Stir their competitive spirit to rank among the elite builders of HGI.

Constant Personal Information

With the advent of technology and the Internet, getting current news and information to large masses of people has never been easier. But it still takes a leader to make sure their team is receiving and implementing this information on a timely basis.

Make sure your leaders are constantly receiving information through every possible method:

- Company events
- The Associate section of HGICrusade.com
- HGIUniversity.com
- Company e-mail
- Company conference calls
- Unified messaging system
- Company mail-outs
- And all other communication vehicles
- You must also use all of these same tools for your team's communication, as well as personal letters, phone calls, team newsletters, and team events.
- As a leader add all your team members to your LFSMAX system so you can communicate with them via email efficiently.

Constant Personal Education

Leaders must make sure that their team has the confidence and skill to take its game to the next level. You must run a system whereby the abilities required to run the Leadership Format System and to market our products are taught constantly.

Make sure your leaders are taking advantage of every educational opportunity possible:

- Sharing techniques through personal phone calls
- Powerful training classes during your BOPs
- Super Saturday training blitzes
- Local area Leadership Format Schools
- Company-sponsored training meetings and big events
- Online company web training

Empowering your leaders for success is one of the most important roles you have as a leader.

It is critical that motivation, information and education get to all of your leaders on a timely, consistent basis. Great leaders don't leave these critical components of their business to chance — they make it happen.

For training and educational purposes only. Not to be used with the public.

150

Director of Motivation

There are three main areas of focus to build a large organization:

1. Recruit
2. Build
3. Motivate

Motivate doesn't mean you have to become a great motivator. All you have to become is a Director of Motivation – someone who directs their people to the places, people and events that will stretch their vision for them.

There are two things you must remember:

1. People will rise no higher than their level of vision.
2. People will only change after having a significant emotional experience.

Every meeting in HGI should be focused toward this end.

A vast amount of time, money and effort is spent making sure that the major company events create the perfect environment for vision-stretching and significant emotional experiences. Never underestimate the "magic of crowds." What if you missed just one meeting, but it was the one that could have made the difference in making or breaking your career?

You must commit to do whatever it takes to never miss a meeting, and make sure that every member of your team does the same.

You Build Your Business From Great Event To Great Event

You can always measure the success of a leader by who and how many follow them to great events. As soon as the company announces a big event, you must immediately begin promoting it to your entire team at all of your meetings. Lead by example by always being the first on your team to register for every event. Stay aligned with major HGI events by monitoring up-to-the-minute information at HGICrusade.com, and through special mailouts and company email communications.

HGI Meeting Flow

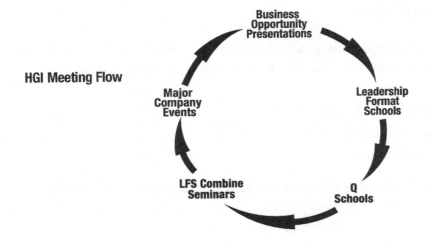

Business Opportunity Presentations

Leadership Format Schools

Q Schools

LFS Combine Seminars

Major Company Events

For training and educational purposes only. Not to be used with the public.

HGI World-Class Meetings and Events

"You build your business from big event to big event."

— Hubert Humphrey, HGI Founder & Architect of the System

Meetings are a critical component to building a big business in HGI. You can tell a great leader by who and how many follow him/her to great events. As soon as the company announces a big event, you must immediately begin promoting it to your entire team at all of your meetings. Lead by example by always being the first on your team to register for every event. Stay aligned with major HGI events by monitoring up-to-the-minute information at HGICrusade.com.

Business Opportunity Presentations

There are two types of BOPs:

- **One-on-One BOPs**
  When? All the time... anytime
  Where? Anywhere two or more are gathered

- **Office BOPs**
  When? Minimum one night per week – preferably three
  Where? At your office or a hotel

  Purpose: To sell the dream to your "old" people, to teach your "old" people how to sell the dream, and to sell the dream to your "new" people.

Leadership Format Schools

When? Every six to eight weeks
Where? Local area hotels/offices

Purpose: To sell the dream to your "old" people, to teach your "old" people how to sell the dream, and to sell the dream to your "new" people on a larger scale with all local area teams.

LFS Combine Seminars (see pgs. 160-161).

When? Every three to four months
Where? Local area hotels/offices

Purpose: To help train all associates and provide the opportunity for recognition on a local level.

Atlanta VIP Red Carpet Days

When? Three to four times a year

Where? HGI Executive World Headquarters

Purpose: To show the power of the HGI opportunity to new prospects or associates who have already attended a BOP and are ready to take the next step.

* Convention of Champions

When? Summer

Where? Varies

* Top Gun

When? Late Fall

Where? Varies

* Company Sponsored Tours and Training – throughout the year

When? throughout the year

Where? Varies

* Company Incentive Trips

"Conquest of Paradise" Hawaii and other luxurious destinations.

* "Search for Alexander"

When? throughout the year

Where? Europe, Asia and other great world destinations

* Major Company Events

Purpose: To provide all leaders with the latest motivation, information and education to help build their business. It is the ultimate environment for vision-stretching and significant emotional experiences.

Keys To "Directing" Your Team To All Events

1. Make sure you and your team make a commitment to never miss a meeting or an event.

2. As soon as a meeting is announced, you must personally register immediately and make sure that your leaders do the same.

3. You must immediately make your reservations to stay at the event's headquarters hotel. The meetings before the meeting and after the meeting are more important than the meetings themselves. It is impossible to get the full impact of an event for you and your team if you are staying at another hotel – even if it's just across the street.

4. You must communicate the details of the event early and often.

5. You must personally call all of your leaders to make sure they are committed to attend.

6. If money is an issue for someone, you must help them understand that it is an investment in themselves – it could mean the difference between success and mediocrity.

7. You must do possibility projections with each of your leaders to see who and how many they will have in attendance at each event.

8. Run team contests to drive registration and push people to win company contests.

Key Points To Teach Your Team How To Maximize The Power Of All Events — Build A Winning Team Tradition

1 Arrive prepared – attitude and appearance mean everything. Business dress is required for BOPs and VIP Days. Company and team shirts should be worn to other events.

2. Take notes – "what flows through you sticks to you." You must be a student of the business.

3. Arrive early – leave late. Treat each meeting like the Super Bowl. You must be ready.

4. Fight for the front. You must arrive early with your team to get the best seats up front for each session. It is a totally different meeting, and has more impact when you're in the front, instead of the back.

5. Create Team MoZone (Momentum Zone). Commit to be the most excited team at the event. Applaud and cheer for every speaker and award winner the way you would like the crowd to treat you.

6. Keep your head in the game. Focus on what is happening throughout the entire meeting. Do not leave the meeting or hang out in the hallways at any time for any reason.

7. Don't get distracted. You must stay focused.

8. Make sure to have your team recap meeting at the office within the first few days of returning from an event to share the "good news" with people who were unable to attend.

History has proven that the leader who has the most people at the most events makes the most money. Make sure you and your Leaders master the art of becoming a "Director of Motivation."

Leadership Format School Dynamics

"As I look back on my career, the events that had the most impact in my life occurred at area schools such as HGI's high-powered Leadership Format Schools. I never will forget, as long as I live, my first impressions as I went into my very first meeting of this type in Atlanta during my early days at the old Admiral Benbow Inn. I could tell from the moment I walked in that I was indeed involved in something bigger than myself.

I remember how I absorbed like a sponge the simplistic but powerful building techniques that changed my life forever. I can also remember getting my first recognition, and being able to speak at those early schools. What an impact it had on my life…!

It would be hard to imagine my career without Leadership Format-type schools. They are one of the great uniquenesses of our company. For us to continue our incredible growth speed and to reach our full potential in the future, we must redouble our efforts in harnessing the tremendous power of Leadership Format Schools."

— Hubert Humphrey, HGI Founder & Architect of the System

5 Key Points about Leadership Format Schools

1. The main purpose of the school is to share the vision of HGI.

2. Have the most enthusiastic/Do-It-First Leaders speaking.

3. Delegate and share the responsibilities of the school with several of the most serious Leaders to have everyone involved in the success of the event.

4. Make sure you have a first-class location with an electric, professional atmosphere.

5. Include HGI Corporate Executive team and top Super Team Builders nationally, contributing via Skype or Google Hangouts, or Periscope, or other streaming technology.

Leadership Format School Dynamics *(Continued)*

One of the main responsibilities of an HGI Leader is to coordinate and run high-powered Leadership Format Schools. These are the keys to running successful Leadership Format Schools:

1. Hold these meetings every six to eight weeks locally.

2. Provide only company-approved handouts and training materials for key LFS topics.

3. Provide name badges during registration for the event (and write first names in large letters).

4. Use motivational walk-in music (pre-and post-meeting and during breaks).

5. Use high-powered motivational banners.

6. Use the latest HGI company image video(s) to add even more excitement to your meetings.

7. Pre-sell tickets through all offices participating in the event.

8. Encourage all leaders to stay at the hotel.

9. Build a team environment to recruit and move people – MoZone!

10. Make sure all speakers are always enthusiastic, always fast-moving and limited to short time frames (five, 10, 15, 20 or no longer than 30 minutes, unless it's a big-time superstar who can hold audience's attention). In addition, all speakers should be well prepared and focused on the subject assigned.

11. Use your best local talent and hottest local Leaders to headline your school, in addition to guest speakers, when possible.
    Speaker Resources:
    - HGI will operate like a speakers bureau to coordinate all guest speakers.
    - Top area Leaders will serve as the hub for speakers on a local level.

12. Harness the power of new up-and-coming stars.

13. Conduct advanced leadership sessions for experienced veterans in conjunction with LFS.

14. The emcee should be very dynamic, knowledgeable, and entertaining with ability to fill-in-the-gaps left by any of the speakers and enhance their message, as well as be prepared to really build up the speakers with powerful introductions.

Leadership Format School Dynamics *(Continued)*

15. All meetings should start on time and finish on time.

16. Implement a standardized awards program, using company approved vendors. It is important to build tradition by using standardized company recognition.

17. Prepare an agenda and use it to properly conduct your meetings.

18. Prepare registration and organizational forms to help you conduct the business aspect of the school.

The Most Important Part of the School Is... "The Meeting After the Meeting"

- Make sure there are plenty of receptions and social events after the meetings to help you motivate and to build personal relationships.
- There is great magic in having all of the local attendees stay at the hotel to create the "Meeting after the Meeting."
- Meetings after the Meetings provide your greatest opportunity for key "one-on-one" teaching, motivation and recognition.

Promote the School to Your Entire Team

- Announce dates and sites as far in advance as possible.
- Promote the event to your entire leadership team and have them promote it downline.
- Promote the event as one that every single associate simply cannot afford to miss, no matter who they are or where they are in the company.
- Challenge your Leaders to get their entire teams to participate in the Leadership Format Schools and recognize the teams bringing the most people.

For training and educational purposes only. Not to be used with the public.

157

HGI Leadership Format School Suggested Agenda

Friday Night, 7 – 10 p.m.
Theme: Passion for the Mission

6:30   Music begins/MoZone

7:00   Welcome & Announcements – Set Tone – Our Mission "To Create More Financially
        Independent Families" Emcee: _____

7:15   World-class HGI Advantage Speaker: _____

7:30   Four 3-minute Speakers: "Why I Joined HGI." (Top earners/recruiters in area)
        1. _____   3. _____
        2. _____   4. _____

7:45   Income Potential Speaker: _____

7:55   Partnership Involvement Speaker: _____

8:00   Keynote Speaker: _____
            Intangibles:
            1. Selling the Dream/Personal Story
            2. Vision/Position & Potential in the Marketplace
            3. Passion for the Mission
            4. Company Strengths
            5. System Whereby HGI Recruiting, Building, Training, Motivation, Sales, Income Never Stops

9:00   Five 3-minute Speakers – HGI New Stars
        1. _____   3. _____   5._____
        2. _____   4._____

9:15   Recognition

10:00   Individual Team Breakouts/Individual Team Recognition (Meeting after the Meeting)

Saturday Morning, 9 a.m. – noon
Theme: "Submission to the System" – Leadership Format System

8:30   Music begins/MoZone

9:00   Welcome & Announcements – Set Tone
        Emcee: _____

9:05   Five 2-minute Speakers – HGI New Stars
        1. _____   3._____   5._____
        2._____   4. _____

9:15   Leadership Format System Flow — Speaker: _____

9:25   Prospect List, How to Develop It — Speaker: _____

9:35   Controlling the Point of Contact/"The Play"— Speaker: _____

10:20   Break

10:30   Business Opportunity Presentation (BOP) Procedures (How to Run an effective BOP)
        Speaker: _____

HGI Leadership Format School Suggested Agenda

Saturday Morning, 9 a.m. – Noon, continued

11:00   8 Speed Filters — Speaker: _____

11:10   Get Started Interview — Speaker: _____

11:30   Keynote Speaker: _____ "Submission to the System"-Discipline-
Accountability - Coachability - A proven, predictable, profitable business system

Saturday Afternoon, 1 – 5 p.m.
Theme: Marketing is the Creation of the Outlet & the Movement of the Product Simultaneously

1:00   Welcome and Announcements — Set Tone
Emcee: _____

1:05   Making the Sale
Speaker: _____

2:00   Product Company Training
Speaker: _____

2:30   Product Company Training
Speaker: _____

3:00   Product Company Training
Speaker: _____

3:20   Break

3:30   Five 3-minute Speakers-HGI New Stars
1._____   3._____   5._____
2._____   4._____

3:45   The Magic of Compound Recuiting
Speaker : _____

4:15   Keynote Speaker: _____ Final Comments/Closing Challenge

5:00   Close

Power Points:

- Tone is everything – Proper meeting set-up, music, banners, stage, seating, quality projector or large flat screen monitor as appropriate for the room, quality AV system, dress, etc. all add or detract from the MoZone.
- Appropriate music 30 minutes before start time and during breaks.
- Meetings are to start and finish on time - emcee should keep all speakers strictly on time.
- Events should be properly promoted with calls and flyers, and tickets should be pre-sold.
- A copy of the agenda should be given to each speaker in advance.

HGI Building Combines

One of the unique dynamics of HGI's "Recruit the Planet" master plan is our powerful Building Combines. These incredible regional alliances allow HGI leaders to combine forces to create "Super" Leadership Format Seminars known as Building Combine Schools. These high-energy schools occur usually on a three-to-four-month basis to give your leaders the additional motivation and information to become world conquerors.

ROCKY MOUNTAIN COMBINE
States
Colorado
Utah
Idaho
South Dakota
North Dakota
Nebraska
Kansas
Wyoming
Montana
New Mexico

PACIFIC NORTHWEST COMBINE
States
Washington
Oregon
Alaska

FAR WEST NORTH COMBINE
States
Northern California

FAR WEST SOUTH COMBINE
States
Southern California
Nevada
Arizona
Hawaii

Pacific Rim Combine
Taiwan
Japan
Philippines
Guam
Southeast Asia
Australia
New Zealand

Latin American Combine
Mexico
Puerto Rico
U.S. Virgin Islands
Central America
South America

SOUTHWEST COMBINE
States
Texas
Oklahoma
Louisiana
Arkansas

For training and educational purposes only. Not to be used with the public.

CANADA COMBINE
Alberta
Ontario
Quebec
Saskatchewan
Manitoba
British Columbia

EUROPE COMBINE
England
Scotland
Ireland
France
Spain
Germany
Poland

MIDWEST COMBINE
States
Illinois
Minnesota
Wisconsin
Missouri
Iowa

CENTRAL COMBINE
States
West Virginia
Michigan
Ohio
Indiana
Kentucky

NORTHEAST COMBINE
States
New York
Pennsylvania
Massachusetts
New Jersey
Connecticut
Maine
Rhode Island
Vermont
New Hampshire

MID-ATLANTIC
States
Delaware
Maryland
District of Columbia
Virginia

SOUTHEAST COMBINE
States
Georgia
Florida
Tennessee
Alabama
North Carolina
South Carolina
Mississippi

Meeting Planner Logistics

Site Inspection

The site inspection should be done prior to signing the contract. The purpose of the inspection is to make sure everything is satisfactory with the facility in regards to your meeting.

- **The Meeting Room**

  Is the size adequate to hold your group? What are your options if your numbers go up or down? Check the lighting of the room, especially the staging area. Will your speakers be well lit or will you have an added expense of bringing in your own lighting? Try to hear the in-house sound system. Is it adequate for your meeting?

- **Location**

  The location of your meeting room is very important. Check what meetings or events will be ongoing during your meeting.

- **Guest Rooms**

  If you will be having people stay at a hotel, ask to see a couple of the regular guest rooms. You want to be sure they are clean and in-line with the rate the hotel quotes to you.

- **The Contract**

  The contract must be in the name of the leader holding the meeting and not HGI or any affiliated companies. This is an enforceable legal document so read it very carefully. Be sure that any agreed request or commitments are stated in the contract or Letter of Agreement. Any of your agreed request or commitments by the hotel that are not stated in the contract are not binding.

- **Meeting Room Rental Rates**

  When you are looking for a hotel meeting room and basically that is all you have to offer the hotel, you don't have much leverage in the negotiation. Because you are operating under a budget, a rule of thumb is $25 a chair. If you are looking for space for 200 people expect to pay $400-$1,000 per day for your meeting space. There are exceptions depending on the area of the country and/or the quality of the hotel selected.

- **Ways to Reduce or Eliminate Meeting Room Rental Rates**

  The most obvious way is through sleeping rooms. For example, if you have told the hotel your meeting will have 200 attendees and through your group, you can occupy 50 to 100 sleeping rooms (25-50%) each night of your meeting, then meeting space should be provided at no charge by the hotel. If you know you are going to have some sleeping rooms, but are not sure how many, ask the hotel to provide you with a sliding scale.

For training and educational purposes only. Not to be used with the public.

162

Site Inspection *(Continued)*

When booking a meeting 4 to 6 weeks in advance, you are probably dealing with space that will go unsold by the hotel. Don't go with the first rate quoted unless you are very happy with it. Tell the hotel you are filling a hole for them, and you would like better consideration for doing so.

While you are on a budget, you need to be fair with the hotel. You don't want to nickel and dime them to the point where the hotel loses money or you become a piece of bad business. Not only does the hotel have a reputation to uphold, but you as the customer, always want to be welcomed for future meetings.

Key Points to Remember

• Guest Speakers

Contact your guest speakers as soon as you know your meeting dates, location and tentative agenda. You need to tell them the topic, how long to speak, the times and location. Remember, use only HGI-approved speakers for your meetings.

• Promotional Materials

The initial step in promoting, informing and building interest in your meeting is through your promotional materials. The better the promotion, the more successful your meeting. The most economical way is producing one flyer or brochure with all information about the meeting to be passed out at all area BOPs and training meetings.

• Registration Forms

The registration form can be one of the most vital pieces to the success of your meeting. It lets you know how many people will be there and you can plan accordingly. From the registration form, you can produce pre-printed name badges, prepare awards lists, guest lists, etc.

• Tickets and Name Badges

These two items can be designed and ordered well in advance. Name badges can be done by a printer, or you can purchase the stick on type and have the greeters fill them out when people arrive at the meeting. Tickets should always be pre-printed and pre-sold. Investigate options like EventBright.com for online event ticket systems.

• Guest Seating

Make sure to designate one or two people to monitor the seating in your meeting room. These people are responsible for adding chairs as the room fills up.

Event Planning Sheet

KEY CONTACT _____ PHONE _____

MEETING SITE _____ PHONE _____

ADDRESS _____ CITY _____ STATE _____ ZIP _____

NUMBER OF PEOPLE EXPECTED _____ SET-UP ➤THEATRE ➤CLASSROOM

MEETING DATE(S) _____ TIME(S) _____

NAME OF MEETING ROOM/FACILITY _____

KEYNOTE SPEAKER(S) _____ OTHER SPEAKERS _____

ROOM SET-UP

STAGE _____ HEIGHT _____ SIZE _____ ➤MUSIC CDS

➤PODIUM W/MIC   ➤CD PLAYER

➤WIRELESS MICS   ➤VIDEOS/DVDS

➤OVERHEAD, PENS & TRANSPARENCIES   ➤DVD PLAYER

➤SCREEN   ➤PROJECTOR

➤BANNER PLAN   ➤TV MONITORS

➤BANNERS/SIGNS   ➤FLIPCHART/WHITEBOARD

➤MULTIMEDIA   ➤LIGHTING

➤LAPTOP COMPUTER & BACKUP   ➤SOUND SYSTEM

REGISTRATION/INFORMATION

REGISTRATION DESK _____

LOCATION _____

➤6' TABLES   ➤EASELS/SIGNS   ➤COMPUTER

➤CHAIRS   ➤WASTEBASKETS

➤BANNERS   ➤HOUSE PHONE

ADDITIONAL AREAS

➤PACKET DISTRIBUTION   ➤VENDOR BOOTHS   ➤SALES ITEMS

OTHER

➤SIGNAGE   ➤DOOR GREETERS (CHECK NAME BADGES)   ➤CHAIR MONITORS

Event Budget Sheet

Meeting Dates _____

Location _____

Planned Meeting Agenda: Event Times:

       Day 1 _____ _____

       Day 2 _____ _____

       Day 3 _____ _____

       Day 4 _____

Meeting Room Expense _____

Hotel Room Expenses _____

Reception(s) Expenses _____

Staff Expenses _____

VIP Guest Air Travel Expense _____

VIP Guest Accommodation Expense _____

VIP Guest Ground Transportation Expense _____

Banner/Signage Expenses _____

Awards/Recognition Expense _____

Printing Expense _____

Staging/Audio/Visual Expenses _____

Video Expenses _____

Photography Expenses _____

Specialty Items Expenses _____

Other/Misc. Expense _____

                        Total Expenses _____

        Conservative Expected Number of Attendees = _____

                   Cost Per Person $ _____

Event Check List

	Contact:	Status:	Deadline:

Hotel
    Inspection _____ _____ _____
    Meeting Rooms
    Receptions
    Registration/Additional

Tables/Booths
    Contract
    Specifications

Room Set-Up Plan
    Audio/Visual
    Rooming List
    Registration Desk
    Door Greeters/Security
    Event Signage/Banners/Entry Decor

Guest Speaker(s)
    Air Reservations
    Hotel Reservations
    Transfers

Promotional Material
    Flyers/Posters
    Registration Form

Printing
    Promo Material
    Tickets
    Name Badges
    Packets
    Additional Handouts

Banners
    Awards/Recognition
    Awards List
    Plaques
    Certificates
    Other

DVD/CD-ROM
    Videos
    Promos
    Multimedia

Planning
    Event Plan
    Working Agenda

World-Class Recognition & Reward System

Hegemon Group International is committed to rewarding our greatest leaders and team builders with one of the most powerful recognition systems in business today. Every new associate has the same opportunity to be rewarded for his or her extraordinary success – with trips around the world and the most incredible recognition program in the industry.

Join HGI and See the World

HGI rewards its greatest leaders with the best of the best in world-class trips. If your dreams include visiting the world's greatest dream destinations such as Hawaii, Europe and the most exotic and luxurious playgrounds for the rich and famous, HGI will take you there in style.

The Achievement System

Every person in HGI – from the newest associate to the highest level of CEO MD – is recognized by his or her respective HGI Achievement System pin. Your upline RMD leader will recognize you at local events as you rise through the ranks on your way to CEO MD.

Builder Pin

Complete field building and field build one new recruit to earn your Builder pin.

RMD

Regional Marketing Director promotion earns the one-diamond RMD pin.

EFC

Executive Field Chairman promotion earns the six-diamond EFC pin.

SEFC

Senior Executive Field Chairman promotion earns the seven-diamond SEFC pin.

CEO MD

Chief Executive Officer Marketing Director promotion earns eight-diamond CEO MD pin.

WEALTH BUILDER
CIRCLE

ONLY HGI's GREATEST WEALTH BUILDERS QUALIFY FOR THE ELITE LEVELS OF THE WEALTH-BUILDER CIRCLE. YOUR RECOGNITION LEVEL IS DETERMINED BY YOUR ROLLING 12-MONTH CASH FLOW.

$50,000 SUCCESS SOCIETY

$50,000+ EARNINGS QUALIFY FOR THE CUSTOM HGI $50,000 SUCCESS SOCIETY WATCH.

$100,000 CHAMPIONS CLUB

$100,000+ EARNINGS WIN THE COVETED HGI $100,000 CHAMPIONS CLUB RING. RECEIVE DIAMONDS ON YOUR RING FOR EACH $100,000 EARNED.

DIAMOND CLUB

$500,000+ EARNINGS INDUCTION INTO THE HGI DIAMOND CLUB AND RECEIVE PRESTIGIOUS DIAMOND CLUB BLACK BLAZER AND PIN FOR THE LEADER AND SPOUSE.

DOUBLE DIAMOND

$1,000,000+ EARNINGS ACHIEVE THIS INCOME MILESTONE AND BE REWARDED WITH 10 DIAMONDS PLUS THE DOUBLE DIAMOND RED BLAZER AND DOUBLE DIAMOND CLUB PIN.

TRIPLE DIAMOND

$2,000,000+ EARNERS BLUE SAPPHIRE RING WITH THREE DIAMONDS, TRIPLE DIAMOND GREEN BLAZER AND TRIPLE DIAMOND CLUB PIN

ROYAL DIAMOND

$4,000,000+ EARNERS EMERALD RING WITH FOUR DIAMONDS, ROYAL DIAMOND BLUE BLAZER AND ROYAL DIAMOND CLUB PIN

WORLD DIAMOND

$5,000,000+ EARNERS RUBY RING WITH GIANT DIAMOND, WORLD DIAMOND GOLD BLAZER AND WORLD DIAMOND CLUB PIN

WORLD CROWN DIAMOND

$10,000,000 + EARNERS DISTINCTIVE PAVE' DIAMOND TOP RING, SURROUNDED BY 10 DIAMONDS, WORLD CROWN ROYAL PURPLE BLAZER, AND WORLD CROWN DIAMOND CLUB PIN

Members of the Diamond Club will also be invited to elite Diamond Club trips and will participate in additional commissions from the exclusive Diamond Club Pool.

How To Qualify

SUCCESS SOCIETY WATCH
To qualify for the $50,000 Success Society Watch, you must earn a rolling 12-month cash flow of $50,000.

CHAMPIONS CLUB RING
To qualify for the $100,000 Champions Club Ring, you must earn a rolling 12-month cash flow of $100,000.

DIAMOND CLUB
To qualify for the Diamond Club, you must have a minimum of 6 direct RMDs or QRMD equivalency and one of the following:
1. $500,000+ rolling 12-month cash flow, or
2. 2,500,000 Super Base-1st Gen. Business Value AV – rolling 12 months, or
3. 5,000,000 Super Team-6th Gen. Business Value AV – rolling 12 months

MEMBERSHIP BENEFITS
- Special recognition at company events including enhanced rings, distinctive blazers, and Diamond Club pins.
- Additional points toward Equity Sharing Credit Pool
- Diamond Club retreats to the great destinations of the world..

DOUBLE DIAMOND
To qualify, you must have a minimum of 6 direct RMDs or QRMD equivalency and one of the following:
1. $1,000,000+ rolling 12-month cash flow, or
2. 5,000,000 Super Base-1st Gen. Business Value AV – rolling 12 months, or
3. 10,000,000 Super Team-6th Gen. Business Value AV – rolling 12 months

Triple Diamond, Royal Diamond and World Diamond members participate in both the Diamond Club and Double Diamond Pools in addition to receiving extra, special recognition.

TRIPLE DIAMOND
To qualify, you must have a minimum of 6 direct RMDs or QRMD equivalency, one of the following:
1. $2,000,000+ rolling 12-month cash
2. 10,000,000 Super Base-1st Gen. Business Value AV – rolling 12 months
3. 20,000,000 Super Team-6th Gen. Business Value AV – rolling 12 months

ROYAL DIAMOND
To qualify, you must have a minimum of 6 direct RMDs or QRMD equivalency, one of the following:
1. $4,000,000+ Rolling 12-month cash flow
2. 20,000,000 Super Base-1st Gen. Business Value AV – rolling 12 months
3. 40,000,000 Super Team-6th Gen. Business Value AV – rolling 12 months

WORLD CROWN DIAMOND
To qualify, you must have a minimum of 6 direct RMDs or QRMD equivalency, one of the following:
1. $10,000,000+ rolling 12-month cash flow
2. $50,000,000 Super Base-1st Gen. Business Value AV — rolling 12 months
3. $100,000,000 Super Team-6th Gen. Business Value AV — rolling 12 months

EXECUTIVE LEADERSHIP CABINET

Always committed to finding new ways to improve the quality of the HGI opportunity, Hubert has formed the HGI Executive Leadership Cabinet. The ELC will be reconstituted every six months by inducting new members who rank in the top of their respective groups:

- Top 10 Board of Advisors Members
- Top 5 Executive Council Members
- Top 10 Director's Club Members

Rankings will be determined by adding monthly golf scores for the six-month qualifying period. All members will attend exclusive ELC meetings, participate in ELC conference calls with Hubert Humphrey and receive custom ELC logo shirts, jackets, portfolios and much more. Receive additional points toward Equity Sharing Credit Pool.

HGI CHAMPIONSHIP BOXING BELTS

Hegemon Group International is bringing back a great tradition from the past — Championship Boxing Belts. The belts will be presented to the undisputed champion in each of four different categories. The six-month contests will cycle twice a year, so that the reigning champion must defend his or her belt to retain it at all major company events.

The HGI Championship Boxing Belts will be awarded at the Convention of Champions and Top Gun each year. The Top 10 Contenders in each category will also be recognized on stage:

- No. 1 Personal Business Value
- No. 1 RMD Base Business Value AV
- No. 1 RMD Super Base - 1st Gen. Business Value AV
- No. 1 Super Team - 6th Gen. Business Value AV

HALL OF FAME

HGI LEADERS WHO CONSISTENTLY DISTINGUISH THEMSELVES AS MVP-TYPE LEADERS ON A COMPANY-WIDE SCALE WILL BE INDUCTED INTO THE HALL OF FAME.

HOW TO QUALIFY FOR THE HALL OF FAME:
- 500,000 BUSINESS VALUE AV IN ONE MONTH FROM ALL PRODUCT LINES
- 9 1ST GENERATION QUALIFIED RMDs
- $500,000 ROLLING 12-MONTH CASH FLOW

RECOGNITION: CUSTOM PHOTOGRAPH PORTRAIT DISPLAYED AT THE HGI HEADQUARTERS IN ATLANTA.

HALL OF LEGENDS

HGI LEADERS WHO CONSISTENTLY DISTINGUISH THEMSELVES AS MVP-TYPE LEGENDARY LEADERS ON A COMPANY-WIDE SCALE WILL BE INDUCTED INTO THE HALL OF LEGENDS.

HOW TO QUALIFY FOR THE HALL OF LEGENDS:
- 1,500,000 BUSINESS VALUE AV IN ONE MONTH FROM ALL PRODUCT LINES
- 15 1ST GENERATION QUALIFIED RMDs OR 3 DIRECT EFCs
- $1,500,000 ROLLING 12-MONTH CASH FLOW

RECOGNITION: GIANT CUSTOM HAND-PAINTED PORTRAIT DISPLAYED AT THE HGI HEADQUARTERS IN ATLANTA.

CHAIRMAN'S CIRCLE OF HONOR

THE CHAIRMAN'S CIRCLE OF HONOR IS THE ULTIMATE RECOGNITION FOR THE ASSOCIATES WHO REACH THE TOP. HUBERT HUMPHREY WILL INDUCT LEADERS WHO DISTINGUISH THEMSELVES BY BUILDING THE MOST CHAMPIONS CLUB RING EARNERS, DIAMOND CLUB MEMBERS AND HALL OF FAME INDUCTEES.

MINIMUM STANDARDS FOR CONSIDERATION:
- 10 CHAMPIONS CLUB RING EARNERS
- 2 DIAMOND CLUB MEMBERS
- 1 HALL OF FAME INDUCTEE
- $2,000,000/YR. CASH FLOW

RECOGNITION: GOLD ROLEX PRESIDENTIAL

Conquer Your Future

HGI is looking for the next generation of Modern-Day Alexanders. Like Alexander the Great, whose chief aim was to "Conquer the World and Make it Greek," HGI's Modern-Day Alexanders want to "Conquer the World and Make it Wealthy." Just like Alexander, Hubert Humphrey is looking to build a company-wide group of leaders who are 100% committed to becoming Modern-Day Alexanders to conquer the business world.

Profile of a Member of the Companion Cavalry

- Leaders who are ready to take a big-time recruiting and building charge

- Leaders who are prepared to become bigger stars as a result of being part of the Companion Cavalry

- Leaders who want to build a legacy, like Alexander, to be known as simply "the greatest"

- Leaders who believe in a more noble cause

- Leaders who believe they can change the world

- Leaders who are ready to take the next step... the evolution to Modern-Day Alexanders

This is the official logo of the Companion Cavalry. The Super Team name of your upline EFC or Diamond Club member will be added below the logo.

Two Main Components of the Army of Conquest Master Plan

Build an "Army of Conquest" committed to becoming the next generation of Modern-Day Alexanders.

Main Component No. 1.

> HGI Plan to Focus
> - Focal Point No. 1: Recruiting

Main Component No. 2.

> Wealth Builder Pathway to CEO MD
> — Focal Point No. 2: Building

Main Component No. 1
HGI Plan To Focus - Focal Point No. 1: Recruiting

You must qualify to wear the Warrior shirts. Any leader, regardless of promotion level, who meets the guidelines qualifies. It's never too early to be building your base.

 10 Base Recruits — On track for CEO MD Team "Companion Cavalry"- white Warrior shirt (with Companion Cavalry logo)/Attend their meetings.

 25 Base Recruits — Inducted into your CEO MD Team "Companion Cavalry"- light blue Warrior shirt (with Companion Cavalry logo)

 50 Base Recruits — On track for Hubert's All-Company "Companion Cavalry" - dark blue Warrior shirt (with Companion Cavalry logo)

 75 Base Recruits — Inducted into the "Royal Elite Guard" of Hubert's All-Company "Companion Cavalry"- light green Warrior shirt (with Companion Cavalry logo)

 100 RMD Base Recruits — Become Hubert's All-Company "Modern-Day Alexander"- gold Warrior shirt (with Modern-Day Alexander logo)
Hubert's main Inner Circle of Warriors who will participate in elite Warrior Summits

---

Warrior Circle
- Qualify to attend elite Warrior Summits.

 100 Super Base- 1st Recruits/Mo. — Inducted into Hubert's All-Company "Warrior Circle" - khaki Warrior shirt (with Warrior Circle logo)

 200 Super Base- 1st Recruits/Mo. — Inducted into Hubert's All-Company "Warrior Circle" - red Warrior shirt (with Warrior Circle logo)

 300 Super Base- 1st Recruits/Mo. — Inducted into Hubert's All-Company "Warrior Circle" - black Warrior shirt (with Warrior Circle logo)

Main Component No. 2
Wealth Builder Pathway To CEO MD – Focal Point No. 2: Building

Converting High-Volume Recruiting Into Great Teams

In the Leadership Format System manual, it teaches you about the laws of duplication.

Law No. 1	A recruit is not a recruit until he/she has a recruit.
Law No. 2	A recruit does not become a leg with a life of its own until it is driven at least four deep.
Law No. 3	A leg does not become a team until at least two system leaders have been built in that leg.

This Wealth Builder Pathway to EFC is an instant accountability system. People automatically count their recruiting numbers and direct legs to qualify for shirts and pins.

The pin mark of excellence!

Build wide, deep and geometric for long-term wealth and security.

Base Shop Pins Pathway to CEO MD

1WD = 1 Leg 4 Deep & 5,000 BV/Mo. RMD Base	3WD = 3 Legs 4 Deep each & 25,000 BV/Mo. RMD Base	6WD = 6 Legs 4 Deep each & 50,000 BV/Mo. RMD Base	9WD = 9 Legs 4 Deep & 75,000 BV/Mo. RMD Base	12WD = 12 Legs 4 Deep each & 100,000 BV/Mo. RMD Base

Super Base Warrior Circle Pins

12WD = 12 Legs 4 Deep each & 250,000 BV/Mo. Super Base-1st	20WD = 20 Legs 4 Deep each & 500,000 BV/Mo. Super Base-1st	30WD = 30 Legs 4 Deep & 1,000,000 BV/Mo. Super Base-1st

World Class Support

Hegemon Group International is committed to providing World-Class support to every new associate – including everything from cutting-edge technology to revolutionary marketing tools, and much, much more.

Leadership Central

Hegemon Group International's Executive World Headquarters – also known as Leadership Central – serves as the hub of activity for all HGI associates. Leadership Central offers top of the line meeting rooms.

The HGI Experience is an integral part of Leadership Central, showcasing Hubert's inspirational history-making rise from a leader who capitalized on big dreams to his record-breaking career as the CEO of World Marketing Alliance – and now, to his greatest venture yet, Hegemon Group International.

Turnkey Administration

As important as recruiting systems, product training and leadership are to running a successful HGI business, turnkey administration is equally as critical.

Following all the procedures outlined in this section will assure that you are running a business in total compliance with all company regulations, in addition to state and federal regulations that may apply.

By operating a complete turnkey office, you will be working *on* your business, not *in* your business.

The Power of Building A Successful HGI Office

Whether you are a promising new member of the HGI field force or a powerful field veteran, building a successful HGI office is a worthy, attainable goal. Every dynamic HGI field leader should aspire to grow from a Satellite Center to a customized Super Center. The hub of all business activity, your HGI Office Center is the key for sharing the vision of HGI with the world.

HGI MoZone Centers: The Hub of All Business Activity

Satellite Center

- Month-to-month lease at inexpensive executive office
- Use of common office equipment, phones and secretary
- Professional interview space by day
- Conference room for BOP system by night
- Provides professional business address for mail and/or shipping

Start-up Center (1 to 2 Regional Marketing Directors)

- Size: 1,500 to 3,000 sq. ft.
- No private offices — only multipurpose offices for interviews by day and training classes by night
- Common work room for supplies, computers and files
- BOP room for 50 to 100 people
- Common secretary

Medium-Sized Multi-RMD Co-op/Cluster Center

- Size: 3,000 to 7,500 sq. ft.
- No private offices — only multipurpose offices for interviews by day and training classes by night
- Common work room for supplies, computers and files
- BOP room for 100 to 250 people
- Additional training room for 50 to 100 people
- Administrative staff of two to three people

HGI MoZone Centers *(Continued)*

Super MoZone Center

- Size: 7,500 to 20,000 sq. ft.
- Private offices for EFC-type leaders only
- Several multipurpose offices for hiring interviews by day and training classes by night
- Common work room for supplies, computers and files
- BOP room for 250 to 500+ people
- Three or four large training rooms that will hold 50 to 100 people each
- Administrative staff of three to five people
- Arrangements with off-duty police officer on BOP nights to control traffic

Setting Up the Prototype Center

Location Is Everything

A major priority in setting up the prototype center is finding the right location. Remember, your location is critical to setting the standard for the professional image you must establish and maintain. For that reason, you must choose the right part of town — remember, we recruit to an environment.

Supplies

It's also important to have the proper storage of the required supplies, which are available from the HGI Success Store. All supplies — sales and recruiting brochures and related materials, business cards, books and manuals, DVDs, etc. — must be ordered directly from the HGI Success Store. Inventory of these items is optional, but every center should be fully stocked with all necessary forms and materials for recruiting and sales.

Library

You should also maintain a library with binders containing all information and memos from mailouts that is accessible to everyone in your office. Remember, you are responsible for passing along critical information to your entire team.

Leaders should also provide an accessible library for use by all associates that includes samples of the following:

- All HGI marketing, recruiting and training print materials
- All preferred company marketing and training print materials
- All HGI marketing, recruiting and training links (HGIUniversity.com)
- All HGI Leadership Live shows on the HGI website (www.HGICrusade.com)
- Company-approved HGI business cards
- HGI Achievement System Pins

All of these items and much more can be ordered from the HGI Success Store at HGISuccessStore.com

For training and educational purposes only. Not to be used with the public.

176

HGI MoZone Centers *(Continued)*

Equipment

You need an adequate multiline phone system with speaker phones or equivalent VOIP phone system to handle your anticipated volume of calls. An answering machine or answering service is necessary for handling calls after normal business hours. You also need a reliable, high-quality copy machine so that you can duplicate materials for your associates on a timely basis, as well as maintain good records.

- You also need a desktop or laptop, network computers and printers. The bigger offices will have additional computer(s) for their online sign-ups, computer-based training and much more.

- Top Leaders will also be equipped with multimedia desktop projectors for the ultimate visual display for meetings and training.

- A projector and screen or large flat screen monitor is also critical for BOP presentations, in addition to a stereo system for walk-in music.

- The training room(s) and/or library should also be equipped with a flat screen monitor with high-speed Internet access so laptop or tablet computers can access the HGI online video library.

Office Decor

Suitably framed company posters, brochures and announcements, in addition to awards, should line the walls of your office. A complete series of custom HGI posters is available from the HGI Success Store (HGISuccessStore.com), along with photos from all company events. Take note of the HGI Executive World Headquarters when you are in Atlanta for the VIP Day. Your office should be the foundation for your recruiting activity — so, just like yourself, it must look the part. Use furniture that will reflect the caliber of our business. Activity boards should be in place to track weekly and monthly progress and activity of all leaders in recruiting and production. A separate board should track new associates. Additional office decoration is encouraged to enhance the professional image and spirit of your center.

HGIU Offers a Turnkey Training System

HGI University offers associates a powerful turnkey training system covering all aspects of running an HGI business. The courses are available in several formats, so you pick the type of course you want to take and where and when. With live symposiums utilizing streaming video and audio online, there's a format to fit your schedule.

Plus, each course is divided into smaller units with an average length of just 15-30 minutes. That makes them convenient for both personal training and to use as classes with your team each week. It's duplication at its best.

The convenience of HGIU and the streamlined curriculum will help you run a training system throughout your hierarchy, bringing your new associates up to speed quickly and keeping your existing team members on the cutting edge of the systems and tools that are available.

Make sure every team member is trained on how to login to HGIUniversity.com and is proficient in how the HGI training material is orgainized there.

Leadership Format System

Learn from the master copy himself: Hubert Humphrey teaches the key fundamentals of the Leadership Format System.

Field Building Certification Program

Master the art of Field Building covers the four responsibilities of the Field Builder – making it easy for you to train other field builders, mastering the important step of duplication.

The HGI Success Store

The HGI Success Store is the only place to find everything you need to build your business. The HGI Success Store offers you one-stop shopping for all of your business tools – whether it's world-class brochures, logo specialty items, business cards, or a case of brochures for the Video Drop System. Visit HGISuccessStore.com to browse your online success catalog:

"The Secrets of Money" Brochure
The key component of "The Play" is the "Secrets of Money" brochure – available through the HGI Success Store. The brochure is available with one click in the Success Store. Order your 10-pack to start running "The Play" today.

Print Materials
Leadership Format System tools and a wide range of brochures and posters designed to help you build your business, including:

- Leadership Format System (LFS Manual) & Unlocking the Secrets of the System
- "The Play" brochure
- Leaders With Vision (BOP Flip Chart)
- Magic of Compound Recruiting Classic Book
- Updated "Leverage Winds of Fortune" and "How to Win The Money Game" brochures for your BOP Decision Kits
- Infinity Compensation & Recognition System
- Recruiting, Building and Sales brochures
- And much, much more

Business Cards
This is the only place you can order official, company-approved business cards for Hegemon Group International.

Apparel and Promotional Items
Visit the apparel section for exclusive company shirts and caps, and click on the promotional items tab for marketing tools, such as — note pads, ink pens and logo apparel, and much more.

Posters, Photos, Banners and Signage
This is the place to shop for office décor that motivates and decorates. Take your office to the next level with the Hegemon Group International Success Poster Series. These dynamic full-color posters are available in two standard sizes and are ready to be framed to fit your office décor. Plus, you can order your own custom HGI banners and signage.

Achievement
Recognize members of your team when they earn promotions:

- Warrior Shirts and Pins
- Achievement System Pins
- Champions Club Spouse Rings
- Success Society Spouse Watches

For training and educational purposes only. Not to be used with the public.

179

Section III — DIRECTOR OF MOTIVATION

Cutting-Edge Technology

HGICrusade.com has a brand new look and now includes powerful new tools - like the LFS Team Manager, the cutting-edge team management tool. And now, with just one click, you have immediate access to information for each of the product provider companies. The tools you need are right at your fingertips when you login to the Dashboard Section of HGICrusade.com.

This dynamic website features:
- The latest company news and information
- Downloadable tools such as presentations, business forms, handouts and much more
- Event registration
- Event and webinar calendars
- Leader Scoreboard Live
- Links to the Field Support Desk
- 24/7 HGIU Online Training Videos on Demand at HGIUniversity.com
- The current Field Manuals and other Policy & Procedures Manuals
- Leadership Live
- And more…

HGI - Leadership Center

Now, with just one touch of a button, you can find everything you need to focus on building your HGI business, including:
- BOP Presentation
- Event Registration
- Forms Library
- Field Manual

Scoreboard

This is the place to find out where you and the members of your team stand. Review the latest:
- Contest Standings
- Leaders' Bulletins
- Recognition and Reward System

LFS Team Manager

This exciting software tool provides you with cutting-edge technology so you can manage your team's activity, in all aspects of your business, including:
- Downline Management Tools
- Commission Statements
- Product & Cash Flow Reports & Charts
- Downline Contact Information and Search Tools
- Prospect & BOP Tracker

Open your window to the world by visiting the associate section of HGICrusade.com today.

HGI Personal Website Packages

Silver (IVO) Package ($29.95 month)

With the Silver IVO Package, you will be able to recruit and build an organization, sell HGI products, earn override commissions, and participate in all HGI bonuses and contests and be able to receive promotions to the highest company levels.

With the Silver IVO Package, you will receive:

- Full HGI Business Website,
- Full IVO Communication Tool (Internet Video Overlay)
- Personal Landing Pages and Click-to-Connect Technology
- Full Back office system with Hierarchy tracking
- Access to HGI University Training
- Access to special conference calls and training events
- Ability to compete for special awards and luxury trips
- Participate in special big money bonuses and perks.

Gold (LFSMAX) Package ($99.95 month)

LFSMAX is a system designed to help agents automate an HGI email marketing campaign. It allows you to load all your existing contacts into the system and then introduce them to the HGI opportunity through an ongoing drip campaign and track their interest by how they respond. The LFSMAX system will identify prospects that are highly engaged with your campaign allowing you to focus on those most likely to have interest in joining your team. This online approach to the Leadership Format System will put your recruiting in overdrive and allow you to efficiently monitor and manage your leads.

As an HGI Gold Associate you qualify to earn commissions on other members of your team who are also HGI Gold Associates. The monthly subscriptions from your team members are commissionable in the HGI Infinity Compensation Program. With just a few team members using the LFSMAX system your monthly subscription will be more than paid for. Plus your team will grow at warp speed with everyone using LFSMAX.

With the Gold LFSMAX Package, you will receive:

- All the Silver IVO Package features
- 7 personalized webpages (landing pages)
- 3 pre-written email campaigns with over 40 emails to keep you in constant communication with your recruiting prospects
- A separate set of emails and rules to automate the process of using LinkedIn for Friendship Farming and Friendship Borrowing
- Numerous 1-click emails to communicate effectively to your recruiting prospect pipeline.
- All the features of the Premier version of LeadOutcome (a $60 monthly value alone) including room for up to 10,000 leads, and unlimited email broadcasts
- Your own lfsmax.com email address
- Collect more names faster ... No more manual paper lists that *"never seem to get done"*

Gold (LFSMAX) Package ($99.95 month) (continued)

- Contact leads with no work on your part ... Automation should save work, *you have better things to do.*

- Learn instantly who has become a hot lead – stop wondering who has read your emails, or visited your website ... LFSMAX always is watching *and logs all lead activity ... no more surprises.*

- Always know what the next thing you need to do to succeed ... stop wasting time on email and social media, LFSMAX zeros in on the best use of your time ... **Hint:** you still need to call people, *just not people who will be wasting your time.*

- Make sure your promises are kept with your leads and prospects – LFSMAX has a scheduler that keeps your tasks on target *ALWAYS.*

- Automate all follow-up steps so leads signal you when they are ready to talk ... Finally you will know in advance who is ignoring you (some always will) and who is hearing your message ... *build your strategy to focus on these people and teach your team the same.*

- Use a single click to instantly contact all your leads or a focused group of leads – **Mass Messaging Made Manageable**

- Personalize a special message for your best leads – spend extra effort on your best leads, you can afford to *because LFSMAX tells you exactly who they are.*

- Add contact forms to your websites and social media pages so they work for you 24-7 -- too much money is spent driving traffic to websites, with a lead capture form on your site you grab their email. *Don't just hope they see your website and call you.*

- Never lose a business card or fail to send an initial contact to a new lead -- Amazing LFSMAX lead entry form will work fine on your mobile phone. **Just met a new lead?** *Put the info in your phone and they have your first email when they get home.*

- Use surveys to find out what your lead really wants and then give it to them.

- Easily design your own email series to promote to a group of your leads. LFSMAX is fully customizable, *apply your personality if you wish.*

- Use the LFSMAX pre-written email campaigns so all the work is done for you.

- LFSMAX hands you the most qualified leads ready to answer their questions. **Limited time for the business?** *LFSMAX is your new essential tool to leverage your valuable time resources.*

- LFSMAX uses "Active Lead Intelligence" so you know exactly what your lead wants now. *It's actually fun to see what your leads are reading and clicking on.*

- Powerful marketing technology works in the background yet remains simple to use. Have some tech challenged team members? ... *no worries, LFSMAX is powerful but designed to be oh so simple to use.*

- LFSMAX PowerPages always present a professional image of you and your business

- You can customize LFSMAX for your own voice, or start fast with our pre-written campaigns. LFSMAX is ready to go out of the box.... *Simply add names, press button, watch.*

HGI Advertising

Advertising can add to the success of your business. It can help expand and spread the message. Although it will never replace the one-on-one contact that results in true production and building, advertising can be of assistance. Hegemon Group International has developed ads that will help build your business. Guidelines for using the ads are listed below, more details are available on the website.

Print advertising is available for use from the Associate Login section of HGICrusade.com. Several ads are available, but you must have written approval to use any ad. Customized advertising must be submitted a minimum of 10 days before intended use, in order to allow time for compliance and marketing review and approval.

Selecting and receiving approval for an ad is easy:

1. Choose the ad/ads, from the Business Center section of the website, that you are interested in using. Tell us the name and number of the advertisement. You will find this information at the top of each ad. We will also need the size of the ad you want to use.

2. Tell us how you plan to use the ad, i.e., as a flyer, mailer or in a newspaper or magazine and the state(s) in which you plan to advertise.

3. Give us the contact information (name, cell or telephone number(s), e-fax number(s), email and/or website address, etc.) to complete the ad.

4. Complete the Mandatory Disclosure Form in the back office of your website. (We DO NOT acknowledge receipt of Disclosure Forms.)

5. Email your request to: support@HGICrusade.com. (Important: You must have a completed Mandatory Disclosure Form on file with us before your request can be approved.)

Directions on completing and submitting the mandatory disclosure are also available in the Associate Login section of HGICrusade.com, under the business center tab. (A variety of sample ads are included for review.)

What Every HGI Associate Should Know About Compliance

Suitability ... then Sales!
Recruit ... then Supervise!

In order to protect and better serve the interests of consumers, the insurance industry is one of the most carefully regulated in the United States.

The standards required for proper selling are spelled out in detail by various regulatory agencies and are easy to follow. Failure to strictly comply with the rules and regulations of the Insurance Departments of various states can result in fines, censure, etc. and may result in even more serious consequences, such as permanent disbarment from engaging in the sale of insurance. HGI and our great field leaders continue in our commitment to be the best first, then be first.

As an Associate of HGI, You Should Always Keep in Mind the Following:
HGI Corporate Compliance Policy

We believe that compliance is as important as any other aspect of our business. We believe that dealing in a fair, open, honest and ethical manner will always benefit the client and the company. We believe that maintaining our integrity with our clients will always be our strongest marketing tool.

Unlicensed Associate

Drive prospects to your websites by:

- Utilizing our Advertising Library and your web address
- Use our approved banners and links to drive traffic from other sites
- Get listed on search engines

From day one of your HGI career, it is critical to understand your role in proper compliance.

Do:

- Ensure prompt submission of recruit's Associate Membership Agreement and Licensing Kit to the Home Office.
- Follow the Leadership Format System in building your HGI business.
  Follow the Training and Expense Reimbursement program as published by the Home Office.
- Obtain all materials, including business cards and stationery, from the HGI Communication Center in your back office.
- Report immediately all contact by regulatory authorities to HGI Compliance Department.

DO NOT:

- Discuss, market or sell any product until properly licensed, registered and appointed.
- Misrepresent the HGI income opportunity by exaggerating or guaranteeing potential earnings to new recruits.
- Make promises/agreements outside the promotions guidelines. Do not manipulate the submission of applications for promotion purposes.
- Require or imply that a new recruit must purchase a HGI product or service as a condition to affiliation with HGI.
- Imply or represent yourself as a licensed associate of any HGI company until you have obtained the necessary licenses and official notification.

Licensed Associate

All licensed associates must follow all of the sales compliance procedures of an unlicensed associate plus many more.

DO:

- Once fully licensed, only accept compensation from the following:
  1. Commissions on personal production
  2. Overrides on downline production.

- "Know Your Customer" and only market products that are suitable to them. The more thorough an understanding you have of the customer and the customers goals, the better the likelihood of a high level of customer satisfaction. Collect as much information from the customer as possible. The HGI DIME+, Two (2) Circle presentation, and approved data gathering documents assist the associate in developing a customized financial strategy to meet the short- and long-term needs of the customer.

- Ensure that all products are represented accurately and all necessary disclosures are made.

- Properly identify yourself to consumers and the public with respect to the product or opportunity you are marketing.

- Ensure that all products are represented accurately and all necessary disclosures are made.

- Follow the Compliance Format System.

DO NOT

- Discuss, market or solicit any product that is not offered through or approved by the HGI Compliance Department. Such activity could be construed as participating in an unapproved transaction.

- "Bait-And-Switch" — sell what you illustrate.

- Sign as second agent unless you bring a "value added" service to the sale. Your upline Marketing Director is already compensated through overrides for assisting and training all downline associates.

- Distribute unapproved marketing/recruiting material.

- Communicate directly with any regulatory agency (NASD, SEC, Insurance Departments, Securities Departments, etc.). Never initiate any correspondence or communication.

Licensing Requirements

Agent licensing requirements for various products are listed below.

1. **Fixed Insurance:** You must have insurance license(s) with the State Insurance Department and must be appointed with the product provider.

2. **Variable Products:** As of this date HGI does not offer variable products.

3. **Investment Advisory Products:** You must be a registered investment advisory rep with any RIA that HGI is affiliated with now and in the future.

The HGI Success Anthology

suc•cess (s k-'ses) n. The achievement of something desired, planned or attempted.

an•thol•o•gy (an-'thä-l -je) n. A comprehensive collection of literary pieces.

> *"The only difference between you today and you five years from now, is the books you read and the people you meet."* — Emerson

Proof that Emerson's words were more than just passing thoughts is the incredible success story that has unfolded in the personal and business life of HGI Founder and Architect of the System, Hubert Humphrey.

Under the leadership of Hubert Humphrey, many other Leaders have applied the success principles in the following literary works to change the course of their entire lives.

We have compiled excerpts from what we believe to be the most powerful principles on earth relevant to elevating one's desires and dreams into reality.

Although there are many important principles in these works that have helped shape the destiny of HGI, we have listed here the most profound principles from each work that collectively serves as the foundation for the incredible success story that is called…Hegemon Group International.

"Think and Grow Rich" by Napolean Hill…

…taught us the formula for turning our desires into reality.

"The Magic of Thinking Big" by David J. Schwartz…

…taught us that you need not have a great intellect or great talent to be a giant among men, but you need the habit of thinking and acting in a manner that brings success.

"How to Win Friends and Influence People" by Dale Carnegie…

…taught us that people don't care how much you know until they know how much you care.

"Grinding It Out" by Ray Kroc…

…taught us the power of the principles of relentless pursuit and dogged determination in achieving success and pursuing one's dreams.

"The E Myth" by Michael E. Gerber…

…taught us the essence of the turnkey revolution and the power of duplication in exact cookie-cutter style.

"Waging Business Warfare" by D. J. Rogers…

…taught us the power of strategical thinking and tactical planning.

The HGI Success Anthology *(Continued)*

The Alexander Complex...

...taught us that all successful people are driven by a belief in a mission that seemingly will change the course of the world.

The Mask of Command...

...taught us about Alexander the Great, his exploits, and the attributes of heroic leadership and the role that it plays in developing a dynasty.

Peak Performers...

...taught us the common traits of how ordinary individuals can become extraordinary achievers.

The True Believer...

...taught us that once the conditions are right, the emergence of an outstanding leader will spark a mass movement.

Made in America...

...taught us the enormous benefit of establishing a partnership with people as opposed to just being in business with people.

The 7 Habits of Highly Effective People...

...taught us how to understand our own paradigms and more importantly how to make paradigm shifts.

The Winner Within...

...taught us that teamwork is the essence of life.

Although we believe the HGI Success Anthology provides a strong foundation for any individual seeking a higher law of the principles of success, one can become a true master of his own destiny only by studying these works in their entirety.

At the very least, one can gain an insight into what it takes to build a successful business. And it's even possible to become the architect of your own destiny.

Turnkey Mental Toughness

You must develop the turnkey mentality. It requires mental discipline and mental toughness, but once you have it, you will have the ability to run a "calm empire."

The legends of the future must learn from the legends of the past.

If you want to master the art of hitting a baseball, duplicate the fundamentals of Hank Aaron, Ted Williams or Stan Musial. If you want to improve your golf swing, read a book or watch a video by Jack Nicklaus. If you want to be a great coach, study Vince Lombardi, John Wooden or Bear Bryant.

If you want to be a member of the Hegemon Group International Success Society you must repeat the system over and over and over again. But developing a turnkey mental toughness is just as important as the fundamentals covered in great detail in the Leadership Format System.

To win, you should have:

- The Tools — the Hegemon Group International℠ contact brochures and videos

- The Techniques — the Leadership Format System Fast Track

- The Mentality — Turnkey Mental Toughness

You can learn a lot about Turnkey Mental Toughness by studying some of the all-time great coaches. Proven winners may execute different strategies, but they all share common traits, especially in the way they think.

Staying Power

The legendary John Wooden, who never had a losing season in 27 years as head basketball coach at UCLA, holds the record for the longest winning streak in any major sport — 88 games spanning four seasons. In his last 12 years, he won an unprecedented 10 national championships, including an astounding seven in a row. Yet, his approach to winning might shock you.

"Like most coaches, my program revolved around fundamentals, conditioning and teamwork," Wooden said. "But I differed radically in several respects. I never tried to get my team 'up' for a game emotionally, I never worried about how our opponents would play us, and I never talked about winning.

"I believe that for every artificial peak you create, you also create valleys. When you get too high for anything, emotion takes over and consistency of performance is lost and you will be unduly affected when adversity comes. I emphasized constant improvement and steady performance.

"I have often said, 'The mark of a true champion is to always perform near your own level of competency.' We were able to do that by never being satisfied with the past and always planning for what was to come. I believe that failure to prepare is preparing to fail. This constant focus on the future is one reason we continued staying near the top once we got there.

"I probably scouted opponents less than any coach in the country. Less than most high school coaches. I don't need to know that this forward likes to drive the outside. You're not supposed to give the outside to any forward whenever he tries it. Sound offensive and defensive principles apply to any style of play.

"While it may be possible to reach the top of one's profession on sheer ability, it is impossible to stay there without hard work and character."

Focus on Fundamentals

Red Auerbach, who won more games than anyone in the history of the NBA, knew how to make his players focus on the fundamentals better than anyone. The results, never matched before or since in any professional sport, were nothing short of amazing: eight consecutive NBA championships.

"Today's NBA coaches overcoach their players," Auerbach said. *"The game is still the same. Put a round ball in the round hoop. Just focus on that — not a bunch of complex thinking.*

"The great players, the more you pay them, the greater they play and the prouder they are."

Like Wooden, Auerbach never used the highly emotional, motivational approach during halftime. Instead he was always clear and concise on the fundamentals. If the team had finished a good half, he would reinforce the reasons why. If the players had strayed off course, then he would refocus on what they needed to do.

Auerbach didn't have to kick his players in the rear or juice them up with rah-rah talk. The players knew the Celtics' system and the championship level to which they were accustomed to playing.

The Celtics had the inner-confidence to motivate themselves. The players knew they had the winning system. They had exercised the discipline to run the plays. The players mastered the system to keep them at their high level of greatness.

Auerbach taught them so well — and so much — that the system became a repetitious habit. The players had the confidence; they needed Auerbach to put them back on course if they strayed from the system. That motivated them.

The Standards of Excellence

Indiana basketball coach Bobby Knight, the noted disciplinarian, has been to the NCAA championship game three times — and his teams won all three times. He demands a lot from his players, but the price they pay is worth it.

Bobby Knight's Standards for an Indiana Basketball Player:

"I decided that we had better put together an idea of what we were going to need to win," Knight said. "The first thing that we had to structure was the kind of person we were going to win with."

- An Indiana basketball player can be any size, shape or color. There is no common denominator except for a love for the game and a desire to get the most out of his abilities. He is not only proud of his strengths, but understands his weaknesses. He is first of all concerned with the good of his team, and knows that individual recognition will come through team excellence.

- An Indiana basketball player must have the enthusiasm of an evangelist, the heart of a warrior and the discipline of a monk, and never loses the honesty and character of a little boy. He appreciates the support of thousands of fans, but he is much more aware of the example he is setting for some small boy on the sidelines. He is happy when he scores a basket, but never forgets it was a teammate who passed him the ball, enabling him to do so. While he never lets up at either end of the floor, the other team is not his real opponent. It is the full extent of his own potential that he is always playing against. He lets the referees, with occasional assistance from his coach, do the officiating.

- An Indiana basketball player is made, not born. He is constantly striving to reach his potential, knowing that he will bypass others who cannot withstand the strain in this quest for excellence. He realizes that the challenges and competition of today's games will better prepare him for tomorrow's world. He knows that the true measure of his performance is not recorded in wins and losses, but how much of himself he has given to the game.

- An Indiana basketball player never realizes when the odds are stacked against him. He can be defeated only by a clock that happens to run out of time. He is what a small boy wants to become, and what an old man can look back with great pride that he once was.

"If we can play in our business with people that have these ideals and goals in mind, I think that we can succeed in any business with those same kinds of people.

"I think that once we decided what kind of people we were going to win with, then I think we have to make the most out of time. I don't think that you or I have any greater enemy than time. We have got to learn how to master time, we've got to learn how to fight it, we've got to try to defeat it — it's an elusive opponent, it's a tough opponent, and we don't always win. But if we're going to be successful, we do have to defeat time."

You've Got to Pay the Price

The incomparable Vince Lombardi, whose winning percentage ranks No. 1 in the history of the NFL, won five league titles and the first two Super Bowls. Everybody knew where he stood on winning.

"Winning is not a sometime thing; it's an all-the-time thing. You don't win once in a while, you don't do things right once in a while, you do them right all the time. Winning is a habit.

"Running a football team is no different from running any other kind of organization — an army, a political party, a business. The principles are the same. The object is to win — to beat the other guy.

"... I've never known a man worth his salt who in the long run, deep down in his heart, didn't appreciate the grind, the discipline. There is something in good men that really yearns for, needs, discipline and the harsh reality of head-to-head combat.

"... I firmly believe that any man's finest hour – his greatest fulfillment to all he holds dear – is that moment when he has worked his heart out in a good cause and lies exhausted on the field of battle — victorious."

The Bottom Line

The common thread between these legendary winners is a mental toughness, a total mind-set about winning. While some of them might have slightly different approaches, their objectives remained the same.

The bottom line is that great teams don't need a lot of hoopla. The ones that do don't stay great for very long. Those who ride an "emotional roller-coaster" will find that it's very difficult to stay on top — and once you hit the bottom, it's very hard to climb back up.

The greatest motivation comes from:

- Self-Confidence
- Self-Esteem
- Know-How
- A System of Accountability
- Repetition—"Relentless Inevitability"
- A Plan that Works

You also need a Socrates/Plato relationship — a mastermind alliance.

The Habit of Persistence from "Think & Grow Rich"

Use these four steps to develop persistence:

1. A definite purpose backed by a burning desire for its fulfillment.

2. A definite plan, expressed in continuous action.

3. A mind closed tightly against all negative and discouraging influences, including negative suggestions of relatives, friends and aquaintences.

4. A friendly alliance with one or more persons who will encourage one to follow through with both plan and purpose.

Discipline gives you new habits to match the system.

Who motivates the motivator?
The Key: He Does.

The Modern-Day Alexander Complex

Alexander the Great's Heroic Leadership

Army of Conquest/Expeditionary Force

Companion Cavalry (Elite Warrior Leaders)
Alexander positioned himself at the head of this battle-winning shock force which would deliver the decisive strikes after initial contact had been made.

Heavy Cavalry (Next Generation Companion Cavalry)
The main body of heavily armored cavalry troops made up the main thrust of the battle campaign.

Phalangists (RMD System Builders)
The feared Greek super offensive weapon, the phalanx, consisted of men of considerable muscular strength who fought in the closest possible formation, shoulder-to-shoulder, armed with an 18-foot spear called a sarissa.

Light Cavalry (Field Builders)
Men selected from neighboring countries for advance scouting missions.

Foot Companions (Constant Flow of New Associates)
Provided solidity to the line of battle to withstand the shock shield while the decisive strikes were being made elsewhere.

Specialist Troops (Loan Coordinators & Real Estate Specialists)
Strategic force that included archers, siege artillery men, engineers, surveyors, supply and transport service men.

Siege Engineers (Headquarters Executive Support Team)
Responsible for planning and executing penetration and destruction of enemy fortresses or other enemy fortifications.

Mercenaries (Product Provider Support Team)
Men recruited from non-Greek countries who believed in the mercenary ethic where professional pride and sheer force of habit worked to keep them in place.

Shield Bearers (Field Support Staff)
Alexander's personal force whose responsibilities included carrying his shield into battle and freeing up Alexander and his key leaders to focus their energies on the decisive points.

The Modern-Day Alexander Complex *(continued)*

Alexander Inc., The Idea

"Alexander's feats defy the skeptics. You can better appreciate the sweep of the man by imagining him in business, arguably the last frontier in today's more circumscribed world...

"His sprawling holding company, Alexander, Inc., would span a dozen advancing technologies, from supercomputers to bioengineering...

"Alexander's philanthropic works might serve as a standard of public-spiritedness for decades, perhaps even generations. So would his reputation for toughness. He inspired men to follow him to the ends of the earth..."

- The Alexander Complex

A Plan to Focus:
Can You Really Focus?
Can you focus 100% to change your life?

The whole focus is **10**. After this, everything else is easy. It's a barrier breaker. If someone can focus on getting 10 recruits, then his/her life will change.

The next 30 days are the most important. With **10** new recruits, you'll have at least one excited person and a miracle will happen.

- All leaders must be sold on the promotion principle. You push and help get your leader to **CEO MD** and you, in turn, will have his/her help and the help of your team when you make your drive. **The Plan to Focus** and the **Wealth Builder Pathway** to **CEO MD** should be taught to every new associate from day one.

- Constantly focus your leaders on the recruiting goal for the month and stay on pace **month-by-month**.

- By month two or three, team Field Builders begin to emerge. You will need a minimum of **30 Field Builders** on your team starting with month nine to begin your run.

A Plan to Run – The "Final Battle" Begins

Anyone making a run for promotion to **CEO MD** must meet these guidelines:

- Declare his/her **intention** in writing to upline.
- Have a current rolling 12-month cash flow of at least **$100,000**.
- Be in good standing with the company - and **"The Run"** will be monitored closely by the company for quality and quantity of quality.

The Modern-Day Alexander Complex *(continued)*

The Dynamics of "The Run" – "Kill Darius"…. The Final Battle

- "The Run" is the last **3** months of your 12-month **Pathway to CEO MD**.
- Three key components of your **CEO MD Run**:

    1. **Recruits** –you must have **100 RMD Base recruits** for each of the three months of the run.
    2. **Field Builders** –you must have a minimum of **30 qualified Field Builders**.
    3. **Will to Win** – **"Drill for Will"** is much more important than **"Drill for Skill."**

Capture the Magic of the Plan to Focus
The Four Power Keys:

    1. Standardize your **recognition system**.
    2. Build a powerful new **tradition**.
    3. Harness the power of **new associates**.
    4. Focus on the **main thing –recruiting and building**

Companion Cavalry Goals of Greatness
The great Modern-Day Alexanders of the Quantum Growth Era must strive to build leaders who hit these Companion Cavalry goals of greatness.

2-Digit Recruiters -10 Personal Recruits/mo.
3-Digit Recruiters -100 RMD Base Recruits/mo.
4-Digit Recruiters -1,000 RMD Base thru 6th Recruits/mo.
5-Digit Recruiters -10,000 Infinity Team Recruits/mo.

Leadership Secrets of Alexander the Great

"After four years with an army, Alexander made himself master of a power whose extent and speed of acquisition stand unequaled before or since. In 330 B.C., he had only to follow up his third crushing victory to be acknowledged ruler of lands that covered a million square miles.

"He had become many thousand times richer than anyone else in his world. He began as king of the Macedonians and confirmed himself as master of the Greeks, Pharaoh of Egypt, and by conquest, the King of Asia. But he had no intention of stopping. A year earlier, he had asked an oracle of the gods in the Libyan desert which deities he should honor when he reached the Outer Ocean. The ocean, he believed, was the edge of the world. Already, he aimed to conquer everything until the world ran out."

– Historian

The Modern-Day Alexander Complex (continued)

The Alexander Complex

- Genuine empire builders are **obsessed:** they can no more stop following their dream than they can cease to breathe.
- What distinguishes the empire builders, in the end, is their **passion**. They devote their lives to an **idea** that in time becomes an **ideal**. More importantly, they inspire others to **buy into the dream**. All are out, in one way or another, to **change the world**.
- Examine a genuine empire builder and you'll discover a drive not to compile riches, but, literally, to **change the world**.
- Empire builders above all think of themselves as **visionaries**.
- The Greeks call it **divine restlessness**. I call it the **Alexander Complex**.
- Like Alexander, they **cannot stop**, nor would they want to. They live in the **grip of a vision**. Work and career take on the **quality of a mission**, **pursuit of some Holy Grail**. And because they are talented and convinced that they can change the world, **they often do**.

Alexander's Three Great Advantages
1. A splendid professional army
2. A clear aim
3. Divided enemies

Alexander's Attack Attitude
1. Extraordinary boldness
2. Flexibility of mind
3. Quickness of decision

The Four Phases of Alexander's Action
1. Contact
2. Cavalry engagement
3. Infantry advance
4. Culminating slaughter

The Ingredients in the Personality of Alexander's Generalship Toward Victory
1. Kingship
2. Leadership of his army
3. Management of his staff
4. Mastery of theatre
5. Command of oratory

The Modern-Day Alexander Complex *(continued)*

Alexander's Caution in War

1. Reconnaissance
2. Timing
3. Psychological preparation
4. Tactical method

Alexander's Technique in the Face of Danger – The Essence of a Do It First Leader

1. Reconnaissance and a staff discussion preceded the advance to contact.
2. Then, he addressed his men - sometimes his whole army, sometimes only the officers.
3. Finally, when the light troops followed by the Companion Cavalry had made touch with the enemy's line, Alexander charged into battle.
4. At that moment his power to command the battle passed from him.
5. He lost sight of the line.
6. He lost all means to send orders.
7. He could think only of saving his own life and taking that of as many of the enemy as put themselves within reach of his sword-arm.
8. But the knowledge that he was risking his life with theirs was enough to ensure that the whole army, from that moment onwards, fought with an energy equal to his.
9. Total exposure to risk was his secret to total victory.

Characteristics of a Modern-Day Alexander

1. Discipline
2. Courage
3. Boldness
4. Audacity
5. Loyalty
6. Concentration
7. Competitive Spirit

The Eight First Principles of War

1. Good leadership is the prerequisite of competitive superiority.
2. Maintain your objective, but be able to adjust your plans.
3. **Concentrate greater strength at the decisive point.**
4. Take the offensive and maintain mobility.
5. Follow the course of least resistance.
6. Achieve security by good intelligence about your competition.
7. Make certain all personnel play their part.
8. The element of the surprise attack.

- Waging Business Warfare

The Modern-Day Alexander Complex *(continued)*

The Companion Cavalry Regimen

To become a member of the Companion Cavalry on a CEO MD Team and All-Company level, you must begin preparation immediately. A daily regimen is required that includes:

1. Full commitment to run the pure Leadership Format System.
   - Your goal should be to commit it to memory and execute it daily.

2. Total alignment with your upline leader(s), Hubert Humphrey and the company.

3. Discipline and accountability in all aspects of your life…
   - Spiritual
   - Family
   - Business
   - Mental
   - Physical
   - Financial

4. Dedication to become a student of the business – read daily and master the principles of all the books in Hubert's Success Anthology (pages 186-187 of the LFS manual). Read these four first:
   - *The Mask of Command* (Chapter One, Alexander the Great and Heroic Leadership) by John Keegan
   - *The Alexander Complex* by Michael Meyer
   - *Waging Business Warfare* by David Rogers
   - *The E-Myth* (the original version) by Michael Gerber

5. Declare your intentions to your upline leaders, to your team and to Hubert Humphrey.

6. Report to your upline leaders daily and weekly on your progress.

The Modern-Day Alexander Complex *(continued)*

The Code of the Modern-Day Alexander

- Carpe Diem - Seize the Day

- I will submit to a "Socrates/Plato Relationship" with my upline CEO MD, and with Hubert Humphrey.

    - Teach transferrables.

    - Copy fast.

    - Let your upline help build your business.

- I will honor the "Perpetual Builder's Exchange Concept."

- I believe in "Team Over Me"/I will create "MoZone."

- I COMMIT and SUBMIT to a system of Discipline and Accountability

- I claim as mine "The Ascension & Dominance Plan" - Discipline and Accountability lead to Ascension and Dominance.

- I am the epitome of the "Relentless Inevitability" Mentality.

- I now see that "The World is My Domain."

    - Domination of the Nation!

    - Conquer the Continent!

    - Rule the World!

- I will always be "Better, Stronger, More Fit to Rule Than Anyone Else...!"

- I have "No Intention of Stopping...until the World Runs Out!"

- "I Claim Your Loyalty...I Want Your Hearts...Too!" I promise that I will honor this.

- "Who Will the HGI Mantle of Greatness Pass On To?" ... "The Strongest...!" It will be me.

- I will "Be as Big as My Ideas...!"

- I have forever forged in my heart "The HGI Plan of Battle."

    - "We are outnumbered in every way..., save courage and discipline...!"

    - "Hold and Wait...!"

    - "When we charge have but one thought...'KILL DARIUS' (Recruit and Build)!!"

The Modern-Day Alexander Complex *(continued)*

The Code of the Modern-Day Alexander *(Continued)*

- "To you...and against failure I commit!"

- I join Achilles and Alexander, "If I had a choice of a long life of obscurity, or a short life of glory, I would choose glory...!"

- I will "Be forged with will and strength of belief!"

- I will display all the traits of a WINNER: ENERGY, CHARACTER, INTEGRITY, LEADERSHIP, COMPETITIVE SPIRIT, TENACITY, INDEPENDENCE AND DRIVE.

- I will NEVER QUIT, nor will I want to.

- I will apply the principles of "THE PURE LEADERSHIP FORMAT SYSTEM."

- I will never forget that the world is my "EMINENT DOMAIN."

- This tribute to Enzo Ferrari applies to me:

  - "First he was a warrior, then a prince, and ultimately, he was the King of his industry."

- I am "Like a hungry lion on the scent of blood, I need a fight, a kill, and I need it quickly."

- It will be said of me that I was "Master of a power whose extent and speed of acquisition stand unequaled before or since."

- I will always retain the VISION and sell the DREAM.

- I will never lose sight of our MISSION: TO CREATE MORE FINANCIALLY INDEPENDENT FAMILIES THAN ANY BUSINESS IN HISTORY.

- I am ready to seize the moment. I clearly see that "HGI is like Patton's Third Army - We are precisely the right instrument, at precisely the right moment, in exactly the right place...!!"

    I will...

      - "Plan like Alexander...!
      - Maneuver like Napoleon...!
      - Fight like Patton...!
      - Build like Hubert...!"

- I will Conquer My Future.

Become a System Builder.
Max Out the HGI Opportunity!

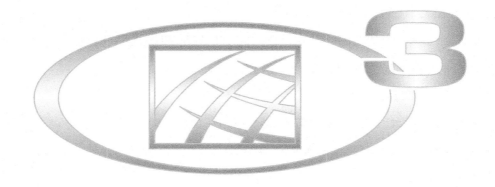

"Your ability to master the Leadership Format System is in direct correlation to the size team you will build and the amount of success you will have."

–Hubert Humphrey
Founder and Architect of the System
Hegemon Group International